The Haunted Tour
of
Britain

West Midlands

The Haunted Tour of Britain

West Midlands

By Richard Felix

FELIX FILMS

First published in Great Britain in 2008 by
Felix Films Ltd
Derbyshire

Distributed by Willpower Distribution Limited
Dalton House, 60 Windsor Avenue,
London, SW19 2RR
www.willpowerdistribution.com

ISBN 978-0-9557535-1-0

Printed and bound by Biddles Ltd, Hardwick Industrial Estate,
King's Lynn, Norfolk.

CONTENTS

ACKNOWLEDGEMENTS

The production of this book would never have been possible without the knowledge and expertise of:

Julia Felix
Daniel Mason
The Maybury Family of Wednesfield
Coombe Abbey
David Lee & The National Trust
New Hall Hotel
Dr. Robert Harris
Dr. David Riley
Chris & Eleanor Thompson
Scott Edgerton
Aston Hall
Dudley Castle
Maggie and Esinah Seopela and the staff at Holbeche House Care Centre.

This book is lovingly dedicated to my wife Julia.

PREFACE

In 1992 Richard Felix decided that his home town of Derby desperately needed a Heritage Centre as a catalyst for him to tell the history of his city, not only to its residents but also to the whole world. Little did he realise what a far-reaching effect the opening of this centre would have and that it would lead to the origins of the now world famous Derby Ghost Walks, that have attracted people from all over the world, which has now established Derby as 'The Ghost Capital of England'.

The walks not only tell the ghost stories of the city but also delve into the fascinating history behind them. Richard is a great believer that ghosts and history go together.

The ghost walks have evolved over the last fourteen years and now offer the public two different experiences. The City Centre Ghost Walk, starting from The Old Bell in Sadlergate, tells the infamous story of PC Moss, the only police officer in Derbyshire to be murdered in the line of duty. After hearing this story it is time for a well earned drink in The Old Tiger Inn before descending into the Guildhall Tunnels - where you might get the fright of your life. The walk continues around the city centre visiting various haunted sites including The Jorrocks Pub, final resting place of a screaming skull. The tour finishes back at the Old Bell with a visit to the attic room haunted by the ghost of a serving maid. The evening concludes with a candle-lit supper in the Old Tudor Bar.

With the success of The City Centre Ghost Walk, Richard discovered another building which was to add to the ghostly stories and tell the tales of crime and punishment in Derby. This was the Derby Gaol, located in the basement of 50/51 Friar Gate. This building was erected in 1756 and was the second of three county gaols in Derby. It remained a place of incarceration and execution until 1840. Richard set about restoring it to its original structure with his usual enthusiasm and expertise.

During the renovation the original graffiti was discovered on the cell doors. These were the carvings of prisoners scratching their initials on them the day before they were hanged. The public are now able to visit the gaol and wander around the cells seeing the condemned cell and the etchings for themselves. The Hangsman Walk was born starting from the Derby Gaol telling the stories of murders, executions and ghostly occurrences. The visitor starts with a brief tour of the Gaol before heading down Agard Street, to hear of the harrowing murder of Eliza Morrow in 1862. Continuing down Friar Gate for the first haunted pub stop, Seymours, there is a picture of the Victorian lady who haunts the pub to this day. The walk continues into the cellars of the Old Friary before returning to the Gaol for supper and then unlike so many others, the visitor will be allowed to return home after making sure that no one follows them.

The fame of these walks and Derby Gaol spread worldwide and as a result Richard came to the notice of the hugely popular Living TV programme 'Most Haunted'. The team came along and carried out interviews, paranormal investigations with the latest hi-tech ghost hunting equipment. On returning to the editing studios they could not decide which part of Richard's interview to edit - as a result Richard was appointed as the resident paranormal historian on the programme - and the rest is most haunted history!

Derby Gaol has now become a major tourist attraction and one of the 'must do' haunted locations in this country. Offering not only ghost walks but night vigils, using the latest equipment and offering the services of a spiritualist medium.

Richard realised how the public are excited about ghost hunting and the history connected to buildings and set about the enormous and time-consuming task of creating the Ghost Tour Of Great Britain. For this purpose he needed a camera man to aid the completion of this tour and this resulted in him joining with Steve Lilley for the production of books and DVD's called 'The Ghost Tour Of Great Britain.' They have now visited over 40 counties throughout England, Scotland and Wales. In September 2005 Richard's youngest son William set up his own production company called 'Felix Films Ltd' which will endeavour to complete Richard's tour of Haunted Britain.

PART ONE

What is a Ghost?

I have been haunted by ghosts all my life, I am not a medium, I am not a psychic, I do not see dead people but I am frightened of ghosts. After years of study and countless fascinating experiences, I now consider myself an expert in the paranormal. I was a ghost virgin until the age of 27.

As a child the very thought of spirits, ghouls and skeletons filled me with fear and dread. I was petrified of ghosts, and to a certain extent, I am still to this day. When I was no more than four I was locked in a huge rabbit hutch in a garage by so called older friends and told that the Green Ghost was going to get me. Experiences such as this only served to fuel an already vivid imagination and as a child I would refuse to stay alone in any building, never venture upstairs without someone's hand to hold and certainly never walk past a churchyard alone. I spent most nights as a youngster with the light on, beneath my bedclothes with my fingers firmly crossed, waiting for that demonic being to appear at the foot of my bed, pull back my bedclothes and reveal its hideous face. Thank God this never happened and it never will but perhaps my way of facing up to my fears was to discover all I possibly could about ghosts and why they haunt.

In 1992 I started to conduct ghost walks around the city of Derby. Fifteen years later, over 200,000 people have been on a ghost tour of my home city. Derby's location in the centre of the country has underlined its importance for nearly 2000 years and contributed to its prosperity. It has always been the crossroads of history. Some people went on to greater things, others turned back, some stayed, some died in battle, others were imprisoned or executed. For these and many other reasons Derby has become 'The Ghost Capital of England, The Dead Centre'.

However, every region in Great Britain has its own folklore, legends and ghost stories and in recognition of this I embarked on The Ghost Tour of Great Britain with a film crew. In the last four years we have visited 40 counties looking for ghosts, talking to people who have witnessed ghosts and visiting haunted places. My experiences as an expert on the popular TV programme 'Most Haunted' have widened my horizons still further and put me in direct contact with some of the scariest places in this country. Even today I am still learning and remain grateful to the folklorists and parapsychologists who continually surprise me with their thoughts and theories.

My quest in life is to prove beyond all doubt that there is life after death and that the dead do return.

Most parapsychologists and scientists don't believe in life after death and put most paranormal activity down to the influence of the living, not the dead. They believe most people are mistaken, overtired, drunk, displaying vivid imagination or are just making it up. They attribute many unexplained events to ESP (Extra Sensory Perception) i.e. the powers of living individuals who have the ability to move items with their minds. At least ESP and the idea of telepathic understanding between living creatures is a more comfortable theory to swallow than the spectre of the dead returning or being trapped on this earth as punishment for terrible crimes through the trauma, fear or pain of an unexpected death.

The idea of sharing our world - sometimes our own homes or places of work with the spirits of dead people is very disturbing, but I have interviewed thousands of ordinary, sane, sober individuals with no axe to grind, who swear they have encountered a ghost. For now please make a note of the Richard Felix rules for ghost hunting. First and foremost you need to be enthusiastic. Second, you need to be a detective and third you need to be sceptical. You have to research and explore all avenues when you look into a ghosts' history and try to get to the bottom of the reason for the haunting.

For most people that would be enough. However, I passionately believe the ultimate aim of the real ghost hunter is to ask: "How can I help"? If you are looking for nothing more than the cheap thrill of a scary experience go and watch a horror movie or go to a theme park. I believe that there is a responsibility attached to ghost hunting. If an animal lover tracks down a caged gorilla, does he simply take a photograph of the unfortunate monkey and walk away? No he does not, that is not enough - the final act has to be the release of the tormented creature from its "imprisonment, pain and anguish". It is therefore important to understand that ghosts- whether the product of the living or the dead - haunt places for different reasons. Some are happy so let them stay but some wish to be released. Their appearance before you, their taps and raps, their moans and groans are all a cry for help from beyond the grave.

So for their sake, in fact for every ones sake, we should be helping them to find release from their earthly torment.

Although I believe in ghosts, I have seen two, heard one and travelled with one. I am still the world's biggest sceptic. I believe that eight out of ten ghostly occurrences can be explained, it's the other two that you have got to be worried about. (The wind did blow the door shut, you just didn't notice that the window was open. The dark shadow leaving your bedroom was in fact your Dad looking for a pair of socks in your drawer).

I have to tell you that much of what folks see, hear and believe to be supernatural is nothing more than a recording. It is not an intelligence and is not self aware. It cannot communicate or interact with you. It is nothing more than a recording. It is no more exciting or frightening than pressing the replay button of a DVD player. Instead of being recorded onto a shiny disc or a piece of plastic tape, it is recorded into the fabric of the building. It's called the STONE TAPE THEORY. Stone buildings such as castles and old halls can hold recordings of tragic and traumatic events. Sandstone especially is an ideal medium because it contains silica, iron oxide and water which is found in recording tapes, and it is my belief that the energy emanates from the stone when atmospheric conditions are right or a person is for want of a better word 'tuned in'.

I believe we all have a pre-ordained moment when we should die. Sometimes by accident this is brought forward due to battles, car or plane accidents, murders, suicides or executions. In fact your time had not come and the energy used by the body in resisting death can be so immense, the electrical impulses given off by the brain moments before death can be so great, that the actual event just before death takes place can be recorded into the bricks, mortar, woodwork and plaster of a building, also into the damp soil on battlefields.

This is why you see the apparition as it was just before death, fully clothed, thank goodness but how can you see the ghost of someone's clothes, sword, bagpipes or carriage. They don't have souls or spirits. The person has to be alive to make the recording. I have recently learnt that the brain continues to emit electro magnetic signals for up to twenty seven hours after death. What about that then?

Seeing an apparition should be no more frightening than watching John Wayne in an old cowboy film. It is only a recording that you see on the screen. He cannot interact with you i.e. 'pop out' of the screen and ask you to put the kettle on. He is not an intelligence, he is just a recording on a piece of plastic tape. In the same way as you play your favourite film over and over again, the quality deteriorates through use. This results in a lady originally wearing a red dress in the 17th Century, fading to pink in the 18th Century, to grey in the 19th Century and finally a wispy grey haze in the 20th Century before fading away completely.

If I was to take you back in time to 1650 and then try to explain how I had been able to record onto a strip of brown plastic video tape an event which had happened months ago (perhaps some of the people at the event may have died) put it into a slot and show you the event again and again on a glass screen, I would have been taken out and hanged, or burnt at the stake as a witch! Today we accept it as the norm; we wouldn't run away screaming "I've seen a ghost". What I'm saying is it possible that with enough energy you can record onto other fabrics as well as CD's, DVD's, photographic paper, video tape, mini discs and magnetic cassettes. In other words, the fabric of a building can also hold a recording.

People frequently report seeing ghosts walk through walls, appearing to be either headless or legless. This is probably because the building has changed since the recording was made. The doorway has been bricked up, plastered and wallpapered. The ceiling or the floor may be lower or higher, the stairs may no longer be there.

Probably the most famous ghost story in the world will explain what I mean. It was the 1950's, young Harry Martindale was a heating engineer in York. He was digging a hole in the cellar of Treasurer's House, a very haunted building in the centre of York. He was alone when he heard a trumpet blast. The mind can't cope with "I've just heard a Roman trumpet". He just put it down to car hooters or a transistor radio until twenty Roman soldiers came through the cellar wall. They appeared to be very small. In fact, they were legless (without legs, not drunk). Harry was terrified, he hid behind some rubbish in the cellar and watched them pass by. They did not respond to him and did not look at him. When they reached a trench he could see their legs. They continued through the cellar and passed through the opposite wall. Harry ran and told his mates who laughed at him, as did many people who heard his rather incredible story. Until one day they did an archeological dig underneath Treasurer's House. There fifteen inches below the cellar floor they found an old Roman road on the exact route that Harry had seen his ghostly soldiers. The new cellar floor being fifteen inches higher than the original Roman road.

No one really understands the immense power of the human mind and how it can react in times of stress, trauma and emotional upset. How many times have you heard stories of super human acts such as a frail woman lifting a car off her trapped child? We call it superhuman strength, but is it? We just do not understand it.

I believe that in the not too distant future we will find a way to unleash recordings of traumatic historical events that lie deeply encapsulated in the fabric of a building.

Although what I have just referred to is only a recording, there are entities, souls and spirits that have not moved on. In death as in life they are an intelligence and have chosen to stay rather than move on. There are various reasons for this. They do not know they are dead, they love the place, house, workplace, person or vehicle and do not want to leave or they are too frightened to move on. The church has a great deal to answer for. It has ruled by fear for nearly two thousand years. Why should he be referred to as a "God fearing man"? Why should we fear God? This is what we have been taught since the beginning of Christianity. The Ten Commandments, Judgment Day, the Seven Deadly Sins, Hell Fire and Damnation have all led to people being afraid of breaking any of these beliefs. If they did break these rules they would be destined for hell fire! So would you risk trying it on at the 'Pearly Gates' to be told "go straight to hell". I know what I would do, I would stay here.

Are poltergeists dead or are they living?

Many poltergeist cases over the centuries have centred on pre-pubescent children especially girls. Examples of this are:- The Schiel case in Germany in the 1580's, the North Aston case 1590's, Epworth Rectory 1716, Cock Lane 1760's, Bell Witch 1817, the Stans case Switzerland 1860 and the Enfield case 1970's.

Most of these famous cases involved taps, raps and movement of objects. In modern times poltergeists have discovered that there is fun to be had with electric light bulbs, phones and computers.

Objects flying around a sleeping child.

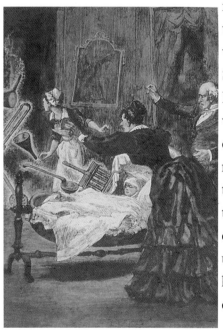

It is possible that a living human not a spirit may be responsible for the poltergeist activity. The term widely used is RSPK (Recurrent Spontaneous Psycho Kinesis).

In a nutshell this means mind waves controlling matter, emanating from someone at or near the outbreak. In other words they are the poltergeist themselves, they are the energy creating the chaos, they are the unwitting cause of the things that happen around them and have no conscious control over them.

The phenomena caused is in some way or other the outcome of a highly emotional state or conflict which has been denied conscious expression or the relief it brings.

In some way emotional tension, anxiety, aggressive urges or

19

suppressed sexual excitement generate the energies which exhibit themselves in what we refer to as poltergeist activity.

A very interesting case took place in 1975 when a new shopping centre opened in Derby. Within days of opening alleged poltergeist activity was reported from various shops. Some of the phenomena were only experienced at weekends when a large percentage of staff were part time Saturday kids. A great deal of joking took place at first but fear soon started to spread. The information was partly suppressed for fear of an adverse effect on sales within certain chain stores.

It was around this time that the city council decided that professional help was needed. All staff were advised to keep a record of events and report any strange occurrences to the council. The outbreak became so serious that exorcisms were carried out in the basements of some shops and Derby Borough Council issued a pamphlet to the shop workers entitled 'Your poltergeist and how to deal with it'.

The following is an excerpt:

A: Its' History
1. *Poltergeists are quite common and have been recorded for many hundreds of years.*
2. *At present cases are being researched and documented in the United States where the work of Dr Rhine of Duke University, and of Roll and the Morrises in England is noteworthy.*
3. *Many people down the ages and many people today, have and are suffering from pranks of their poltergeist.*

B: Its Nature
4. *It is not an illusion and can produce physical effects which can*

be weighed, measured and recorded: i.e. it can move things and it can produce noises...

5. It is attached to and part of the mind of an owner or group of owners...

6. The poltergeist feeds on fear, although it is harmless both to soul and body and is, in its own way, a relief to the suffering mind.

7 Its owner has no control over it and is unaware of his or her ownership.

C: How to deal with it.

8. Once the pressures which have produced it are understood, the Poltergeist will fade out.

9 Where premises have been affected; a ritual blessing will greatly help to calm the atmosphere of strain and fear.

Many members of staff from several shops experiencing the phenomena did make themselves familiar with the pamphlet but it still continued. More exorcisms took place but the poltergeist activity continued for some time afterwards.

Psychotherapy was used on some staff members with better results, which proves in some cases that it can banish poltergeist activity. If it is right to look to the person concerned for the source of the phenomena, then we may be able to discover why it suddenly ceases. Perhaps some change in their emotional or mental state could mean he or she is no longer producing the extra quantities of energy and therefore the rappings, levitations and stone throwing will naturally stop.

In any event, the mind over matter theory is not endorsed by all investigators. Some believe that only a proportion of poltergeists can be explained in this way and the reason that the activity stops is because the malevolent spirit gets fed up, packs its bags and goes 'home'!

Crisis Apparitions

Remember we are nothing but energy. Each one of us emits 2 kilo-watts of electricity each day. We are the best computer ever invented. The more machines we invent the lazier we become. Thousands of years ago primitive man was able to communicate by telepathy, we have now invented mobile phones, but we are still capable of communicating with our mind. The number of times I say to my wife, "get off my wave length, I was going to say that or I was going to phone you". Many stories abound from the first and second world war of soldiers appearing before their mothers or wives and days later a telegram comes to tell them they have been killed in action. These are examples of some form of telepathic link between people who love each other. Sometimes the apparition or ghost as it is called doesn't die. There are various cases reported of ghosts of living people, whose appearance can cause a loved one to summon help, thus stopping a tragedy. Most of us at some time or other get a feeling that makes us visit a friend or loved one who is very ill and we often arrive just in time to say goodbye.

Phantasm

These are ghosts of living people. When the society for psychical research did a survey in 1888 they discovered that many people were able to put a name to the ghosts that they had seen. In fact these apparitions were in no danger and were still alive. We have an amazing ability through our energy to project our image to a place that we would rather be or a place that we love.

There is an amazing account of a baker who retired after many years in the same bakery. After a few weeks his ghost was reported in the bakery that he had once owned. The new owners, believing that he had died, contacted the family only to be told he was alive and well. He had always got up at four o'clock in the morning to start baking and after retirement still got up at the same time. He would go downstairs, make a cup of tea and sit by his gas fire thinking of the work that he use to do in the bakery and somehow through his own energy projected his image back to the place where he spent so many years of his life.

So you want to be a Ghosthunter?

The first thing any Ghost Hunter needs to consider is what is normal, rather than what is paranormal. Most ghostly occurrences can be explained. What does paranormal mean?… It means running alongside the normal. What does supernatural mean?… What we do not understand, we fear. This fear can add to our conception of what we see, enhancing our emotions and reactions. If there is an entity within the building, it can also feed on our emotional fears. When and if something does happen, start ticking off the normal boxes first and if there are any boxes left at the end "whoopee"! you may have found or seen a ghost. The majority of scientific discoveries have been made by amateurs, so there is a high possibility that a ghost could be recorded beyond all doubt by an amateur group of paranormal investigators with the most basic of equipment. This basic equipment consists of candles, torch, tape recorder, thermometer and dictaphone. However, the biggest and most important thing for any ghost investigator to have is patience. Ghosts or paranormal activity does not happen when you want it to. Ghosts do not 'jump through hoops' or perform for audiences. Most ghostly activity occurs when most people are not really expecting anything to happen but they have been emotionally open and receptive to their surroundings for some reason…trauma, excitement, fear and shock. Candles are simple but very effective as they are very sensitive to any slight draft or movement and always create a soft light. This light given off from a candle can be either relaxing or ghostly depending on the mood of the people in the room and how active ones imagination is. Dictaphones and tape recorders are useful but do not

Richard with his dowsing crystal

need to be left recording for hours. They can be far more effective if the use of them is controlled and they are used to record answers to questions, such as "Is there anyone there"? Sitting listening to tape recordings for hours is often soul destroying and impractical, two minutes is quite enough.

Being a paranormal historian I tend to favour the old fashioned techniques of ghost hunting which involves the use of dowsing rods, crystals, tilting tables and even ouija boards (UNDER STRICT SUPERVISION AND ADULT CONTROL). These traditional methods can often give you answers but remember it can only be very basic, i.e. yes or no. The problem I have is whether the message is coming from a spirit which answers our questions, or whether the message is coming from our subconscious… we are without knowing influencing the movement and response of these things. The ouija board can tell us much more than just yes and no. It frequently responds with complete words and even sentences. Do not get despondent if you only get "Gobbledygook" because many years ago the vast majority of people could not read or write and their alphabet was very different to the one we use today.

The question I am frequently asked is "Are ouija boards dangerous"? I suggest that they are only used by people that know what they are doing and do not leave anyone open to any distress or interference from beyond. I do not think there is any difference standing in a circle holding hands asking "Is anybody there"? or sitting around a table asking the same question. If someone is evil in life there is every possibility that they could be evil in death. Using the universal law of 'likes attract', if there is an evil person around the table or in the circle they could attract their own kind. SO FOR THIS REASON I WOULD STRESS THAT YOU DO NOT TRY THIS AT HOME!

Just remember all the scientific equipment being used is only based on us, our minds and brains. We are the best computer ever created and are therefore the best ghost detector.

So at the end of the day all of this equipment can only justify to others that the temperature really has dropped. When carrying out paranormal investigations, one of the most common changes in the atmosphere that people experience is a chill or draft. This can be easily detected by a simple thermometer but even more so by a laser thermometer that will tell you exactly where a drop in temperature occurs. Do remember the laser thermometer will only record the temperature where the tip of the beam makes contact, which is usually the wall or floor. To record the temperature where the apparition appeared, you need a probe thermometer which can be 'dangled' exactly where the activity has taken place.

The trusty EMF meter used by most ghost hunters and waved around on most TV ghost hunting programmes, is not a ghost detector. As far as I know ghosts do not emit an electromagnetic signal. You so often see on TV a medium saying "the ghost is standing over there in the corner" and the investigator walks over to the ghost waving his EMF meter around - rubbish! What you should be doing is waving the EMF meter around the head of the person who is seeing the ghost to check if there is a fluctuation in EMF caused by a badly earthed wire near to them. This can cause a change in the frequency of their brain which could cause them to see a ghost.

When visiting a haunted location I try to interview as many people as possible who are connected with the building. You need to be inquisitive and methodical like a police detective and you also need a confident interviewing technique but one that puts people at their ease. Let them do the talking and record the conversations. However, always make sure you have the person's permission to record what they say. The most credible witnesses are those who live or work in the building as they know the building like 'the back of

The EMF meter

their hand'. They know the familiar and characteristic sites and sounds of the building. You should give more credence to the person who tells you what they have seen, without giving a reason for the ghost i.e. I was told this place was once a monastery and therefore the ghost must be a monk. Beware of linking a ghost of a famous person with the building just because they had an association with it i.e. they lived or worked there. An example of this is Anne Boleyn is said to haunt the area around the scaffold in the Tower of London.

"How do you know it's Anne Boleyn?

Because she is wearing a Tudor dress.

All women wore Tudor dresses in Tudor times".

Anne's execution, although traumatic, was not as grisly as other executions that took place there. If anyone should haunt that area, it should be the ghost of seventy seven year old Margaret Pole. This poor lady ran away from the execution block and the

Richard interviewing Harry Martindale in the cellars of Treasurer's House, York.

executioner chased her around the scaffold wielding his axe until he eventually succeeded in hacking her to death.

Most folks that see a ghost are not frightened when they see them. The mind has an amazing tendency to rationalize what it has seen. It cannot cope with the idea that "I have just seen a ghost"! It is only when it vaporizes or disappears through the wall, the person realises that they really have seen a ghost… that is when reality and shock can set in. Once you have seen a ghost you have to become your own detective just as I did when I saw a ghost in Derby Gaol at three twenty on a Friday afternoon. It was a grey hazy figure, neither male or female, it was in full vision and not out the corner of my eye. The apparition lasted for at least six seconds and I sensed it as well as seeing it. Since this ghostly experience I have explored all eventualities to prove that it was not steam from the dishwasher, smoke from the fire or sunlight through the window, no EMF recording and no infra sound. After eliminating all possibilities I can only come to one conclusion… "I SAW A GHOST"!

If you use a medium during your investigation, either in a séance or vigil, do not fall into the trap that most TV programmes fall into of making the programme into 'let's test the medium'. Take them to the location yourself, do not tell them where your going and make sure someone stays with them. If you have two mediums, try and keep them apart and interview them separately. If they have the same information and emotions in the same areas then you could well be onto something. I believe that the vast majority of mediums and psychics do have an ability. It is a gift, an extension of our five senses rather than a sixth. In the same way as we are all capable of playing the piano but few of us will never become a concert pianist. Some people can even play the piano without having the ability to read music. I cannot play the piano so they cannot but they can prove it by playing me a tune whereas the medium cannot show us the ghost. I believe in ghosts and the supernatural. Therefore I have to believe in mediums. Whether they are communicating with our dead relatives or just have an ability to read our minds. Do they retrieve the memories of our dead loved ones in exactly the same way as the police can retrieve erased data from a computer? Do remember eight out of ten ghostly occurrences can be explained… it's the other two you have to worry about.

Happy Hauntings!

PART TWO

THE HAUNTED TOUR
OF
BRITAIN

WEST MIDLANDS

INTRODUCTION

The Origins Of The West Midlands.

The West Midlands came into existence after a local government act in 1974. It is made up of seven different metropolitan boroughs ----

1. City of Coventry
2. Dudley
3. Solihull
4. Walsall
5. Sandwell
6. City of Wolverhampton
7. City of Birmingham

At the beginning of The Industrial Revolution the manufacturing of goods needed a source of power in the form of coal, coke and iron ore. All of these were found in abundance in this area so urbanisation began which resulted in the large conurbation of industry that we see today. From the 16th Century Birmingham became a centre for metal working industries and ironmongers and the town soon became a centre where guns and swords were made. The English Civil War increased demands for weaponry which brought prosperity through death to the town. The town's people did not support King Charles I and the town as a result was attacked and plundered by the Royalist Prince Rupert. Undaunted the town still managed to produce over fifteen thousand swords for the opposition (Oliver Cromwell.) By the end of the 17th Century two hundred muskets a month were being produced for the government and Birmingham's Gun Quarter was 'born'.

In the first and second world wars the Long Bridge Car Plant switched production to producing ammunition and equipment for the military – depth charges, mines, steel helmets, Hurricanes, Spitfires, and Lancasters were all made. This contribution to the war effort could well have been a major deciding factor in helping win World War Two. However, this victory was not without cost as two thousand, two hundred and forty one people lost their lives and over three thousand were seriously injured. Birmingham has been a city that has witnessed many tragic and traumatic events and due to the nature of its industry has produced some of the finest killing machines in the world. Along with war comes destruction of buildings of which twelve thousand dwellings, three hundred factories and many of the cities fine old buildings were destroyed.

There are two main areas of green belt which manage to maintain their rural character. One of which is the River Thame which is said to be the most urbanised basin in the United Kingdom. This area borders the counties of Warwickshire, Worcestershire and Staffordshire and has a population of around two and a half million.

A settlement of small farms formed the first civilisation in the Bronze Age which was then followed by The Roman invasion that established a large camp called Metchley at Edgbaston. The Queen Elizabeth Hospital stands on this site today. The farming population struggled to exist due to the poor soil in this area of England and this resulted in the land not being developed and remained a 'backwater'. This was also due to the land being densely covered by the huge Forest of Arden. After the Romans left the Saxon invaders arrived who were mainly village builders and the name Birmingham dates back to this time. Its origins came from a Saxon chief called 'Beorma' and ing being 'tribe of' and ham is 'homestead'- which means Birmingham is the home of the tribe of 'Beorma'. The next era was the Norman Conquest and the Lords of the manor were the De Birmingham family. In 1154 King Henry II granted a charter giving market rights to Peter De Birmingham which resulted in the rapid growth of a small farming village into a thriving market town.

Guess what today this is now The Bull Ring! Birmingham is the most important city in the West Midlands and has an award winning water front, state of the art shops and despite its humble Anglo Saxon origins it is now Britain's second city. The great fire of Birmingham in the thirteen hundreds destroyed much of the town and caused many fatalities.

The situation of Birmingham in the heart of the country resulted in it becoming a crossing of the ways which resulted in some travellers staying and setting up home whilst others carried on to new locations.

Coventry was the most important of the cities in the fifteen hundreds but slowly went into decline. However, the town managed to re-establish itself by diversifying into the production of bicycles, sewing machines and cars of which it is still important today.

During the Second World War Coventry suffered much death and destruction during the Blitz and there is an amazing story that most of the cats in the city centre disappeared before the bombing started. To this very day at certain times of the night folk still report hearing the ghostly drone of German bombers directly over the bombed out ruins of Coventry Cathedral. Is it possible that the remains of this building holds a memory of these tragic events and is nothing more than a giant stone tape recorder.

Coventry is most famous for the naked lady who rode bare-back through the city, no less than Lady Godiva. She was married to one of the most famous and wealthy noblemen, The Earl of Chester. He was not the kindest of men and put crippling taxes on his townsfolk. He came to an agreement with his wife that if she rode through the streets naked he would reduce taxation. He did not think for one moment that his modest and religious wife would accept such a challenge. To his amazement on the appointed date she took off her clothes, mounted her steed and rode naked into the history books.

Lady Godiva

Orders were given that folk should draw their curtains, but the towns folk could not resist peeping in the hope to get a glimpse of Lady Godiva's naked body. The Earl was so amazed by his wife's courage that he did not reduce taxes but instead abolished them altogether!

Legend has it that one young boy called Tom, could not resist temptation peeped as she rode by and was immediately struck blind, thus the origins of 'peeping Tom' were founded.

Lady Godiva is not a figment of imagination but did exist and several people in recent times have reported seeing a beautiful lady, riding naked on a white horse through the streets of Coventry in the early hours of the morning.

Wolverhampton was named after a Saxon by the name of Wulfruna who was given lands at Heanton. From this a monastery and a settlement grew bearing the name Wulfruna's Heanton. During the middle ages it was a small market town whose main industry was the weaving of wool. The town suffered two severe fires, one in 1590 and another in 1696. During The Gunpowder Plot two men from Rowley Regis were hanged drawn and quartered in the centre of the city for harbouring some of the conspirators. In the 18th century the main London to Holyhead Road was built and ran through the town bringing with it much prosperity and resulted in the town becoming a major coaching station. With the coming of the Industrial Revolution

Wolverhampton was transformed from a sleepy market town into a large and prospering industrial city.

The city of Walsall started out its life under the name of Walh Halh (Celt's Valley). It became an important industrial centre from the 14th century as coal and ironstone were mined in the area which provided the power and raw material for the metal working industry.

Dudley was a Saxon village, Dudda's Leah (leah being a clearing in a forest belonging to Dudda). This place became the capital of The Black Country and changed from village to market town when the Lord of the Manor established the famous Dudley market.

Solihull means muddy or soily hill. It has existed since medieval times and was founded by Hugh de Oddingsell as a market centre. It became an important coach stop in the 18th Century and is noted to this day for its' historic architecture which includes some fine examples of Tudor timber framed buildings.

The borough of Sandwell was established in 1974 with the amalgamation of the county boroughs of West Bromwich and Warley. It lies right in the centre of the West Midlands. It became known as The Sandwell and the name stuck. The area where the spring still flows is called the Sandwell Valley. With the great abundance of iron ore mined in the area, put it at the forefront of the Industrial Revolution.

That was just a very brief insight of the county.

So settle back, turn down those lights, and let me take you on a haunted tour of the West Midlands.

1. THE ALEXANDRA THEATRE, STATION STREET, BIRMINGHAM

This theatre is housed in a beautiful Edwardian building and can seat one thousand three hundred and forty seven people. The public can come along and enjoy a wide and diverse range of performances from West End Shows, opera, ballet and pantomimes can all be enjoyed in this wonderful setting. This theatre was first opened in 1901 and was first called the Lyceum Theatre. In December 1902 the new owner Lester Collingwood renamed it The Alexandra. In 1935 the theatre was rebuilt in the popular architecture of the day – The Art Deco Style. Today this theatre is one of the most famous theatres for staging performances for children and young people.

The Alexandra came under the ownership of various members of the Salberg family – Leon Salberg and Derek Salberg. It is Leon Salberg, director and owner who is thought to linger in the stalls and

The Alexandra Theatre

wander the theatre. Is he checking out that all is running well in his beloved theatre? A wardrobe master is also believed to have died one evening whilst attending to his duties. He was well known for wearing his carpet slippers for comfort due to the amount of walking he had to do, checking that everyone had all the costumes etc in good repair both in the dressing rooms and on stage. The wardrobe mistress today is one of many staff at the

Leon Salberg

theatre who hears and senses the wardrobe master going about his work. Although the floors are now carpeted his muffled footsteps are heard as if they are walking on the original bare boards.

Theatres, cinemas and places of entertainment seem to attract more than their fair share of ghosts. At the end of every night when the applause has died down, the final curtain is closed the lights are switched off and the audience go home the theatres become quiet and dark. However, this is not for long as this is the time when many of the famous entertainers return from the shadows to perform their favourite part over and over again. Is it the energy of the audience and the players that awaken these ghosts drawing them back to the atmosphere that they once loved?

2. DUDLEY ROAD HOSPITAL, DUDLEY ROAD, BIRMINGHAM

Dudley Road Hospital

Over the last few years during my investigations into paranormal and ghostly activity I have spoken to more nurses than any other members of the community who have provided me a great deal of evidence to convince me even more that there is life after death.

The first building on this site was used as a workhouse and in 1889 it was extended and became the Birmingham Union Infirmary. Florence Nightingale had a configuration recommended by her used in the designing of this hospital.

On one occasion when I was in the studio of BRMB radio station, talking about ghosts, a reporter told me of a story he was told by some nurses he had previously interviewed who worked at the hospital. They described the hauntings of two ghosts that are frequently seen by staff at the hospital. One of these ghosts seen is in the area of the hospital that was once used for isolating patients with fevers. The ghost is described as an attractive blond young lady who is dressed in a grey uniform. She has been seen on many occasions and is thought to be the ghost of a staff nurse who was known to be having a liaison with a surgeon and died suddenly with no logical explanation. Not only is she seen by staff but she has also been seen by patients, who after seeing her ghostly apparition make a remarkable and unexpected recovery.

The second apparition is thought to be a doctor who wanders in and around the area that was once the hospital mortuary. Rumour has it that this may be the surgeon who had the affair with the staff nurse and he is looking for his lover. There is no definite proof that these two ghostly apparitions are connected but perhaps not being able to be together in life, they are still trying to be together in death.

Many nurses tell me that they know when a patient is soon to die. They are able to predict their passing as a loved one who has already passed over appears by their bed as if they have come to collect them. The dying patient smiles and seems to be very happy and soon after they pass over to the next world. What a lovely thought that we are one day reunited with those that we love.

Victorian part of Dudley Road Hospital

3. A HAUNTED HOUSE IN THE AREA OF SNOW HILL STATION AND ST CHAD'S

NOW DEMOLISHED, but the ghosts still linger!

St Chad's Roman Catholic Church

Snow Hill Station

Even when buildings no longer exist, ghostly apparitions and memories still remain, perhaps recorded in the rubble of the building or even in the soil. Such a site is near the centre of Birmingham, in the vicinity of Snow Hill Station and St Chad's Roman Catholic Church. In 1829 the house in question belonged to a gentleman whose profession was to provide doctors with fresh bodies in order for them to carry out surgical investigations for the furtherance of science. By dissecting the human body doctors were able to discover where the vital organs were situated, how big they were and what function they might have. When the patient visited their doctor with a pain they were more able to make a diagnosis, particularly as to which organ was causing the problem. This could be a very lucrative business as doctors around this time were willing to pay up to two guineas for a fresh body. This guaranteed method of making

41

money soon resulted in grave robbing becoming a popular occupation. Bereaved families would often set up a 'vigil' to guard their loved ones body until decomposition set in rendering it unsuitable for the doctors' dissection table.

Cemeteries did not come into existence until the 1850's – cremation was 'taboo'. Corpses were only buried in church yards and overcrowding soon became a serious problem. The sexton (local grave digger) would sometimes rectify this problem by jumping up and down on the coffins already in the shallow grave, crushing them down to make room for others to be placed 'on top'. Little consideration was given to people being 'laid to rest'. Body snatching was not considered to be a criminal offence but the stealing of the bodies clothing or shroud was. Body snatchers or 'resurrection men' overcame this problem by undressing the stolen body, returning its clothing or shroud to the empty grave. Children were often used in grave robbing as they were able to climb into a small chute going down to the head of the coffin which had been excavated to gain access to the body. The children had to climb down into these holes and smash the coffin lid and attach a rope to the body's neck, which enabled the dead body to be hauled to the surface. Imagine the dreams that these children experienced when they closed their eyes to sleep at night!

This method of earning 'easy' money led folk to find a faster way of acquiring bodies - the grisly answer was to murder people to order. The demand by doctors for dead bodies was never fulfilled until the 1830's when a law was introduced, giving permission for bodies from the work house to be dissected for the furtherance of science - there was no restriction on age so children's bodies were also used.

The Royal College of Physicians in London was allowed by Royal assent to have the bodies of six men from the gallows each year. All dissections that took place around the country were usually carried out publicly in the Shire Hall. The hangman would frequently supplement his wages by selling off the bodies of the poor folk he had cut down from the gallows. Around this time the crimes for which you could be hanged were reduced and such offences as walking on the street with a sooty face,

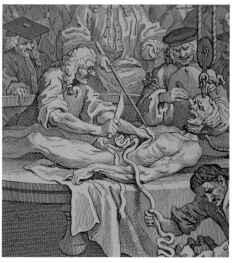

A public dissection

house breaking, stealing a sheep, were removed from the statute books. This resulted in even less corpses being made available for scientific research. Gaols were pleased to send their executed victims for dissection as it saved them the trouble of having to dispose of the body. However, it was not always the hangman that profited from an execution, but sometimes the victim or their family made financial gain. A few men chose to sell their own condemned bodies before their execution. Such a man was John Fontenoy who asked a surgeon to buy his body so he could pay his prison expenses. In 1740 William Duell was hanged at Tyburn and was then taken to the Shire Hall. Just as the surgeon was about to dissect his body the audience heard him groan. He was alive! The same surgeon who was about to dissect him gave him medical aid and he survived. William was not sentenced to be hanged again, but instead was transported for life. I certainly believe that the poor fellow earned his reprieve from the gallows. Life in olden days was often harsh but folk were far more frightened by the thought of what was to become of them in the 'after life' than what they had to deal whilst still alive.

When the house was inhabited, before its demolition ghostly

sightings and sounds were reported by the occupants - who never stayed for long! People walking in this area often hear horrific screams coming from the sight where the house once stood. Are they the last cries of the people lured into this house not realising the grisly fate that was to befall them when the front door closed behind them!

The site of the murder house.

4. CURDWORTH VILLAGE
Eight miles from Birmingham

In this village is found a Norman Church that has 'witnessed' many traumatic and sad events. During The English Civil War many Parliamentary and Royalist soldiers died in the surrounding area and were buried alongside one another in the church yard. Not only bodies were buried but rumour has it that Royalist treasure was also hidden in the grave yard. If there was buried treasure in the grave yard what better way to keep 'gold diggers' out than by inventing frightening tales of headless figures haunting the area when darkness falls. The headless figures were said to be guarding the Royalist treasure, so if folk came in search they might find more than they bargained for.

The main ghostly apparition seen in and around this church is a lady said to be wearing a green dress. What self respecting ghost would want to haunt a damp, cold graveyard? The young lady is reported to be looking at the head stones as though searching for a loved ones grave. Legend has it that she is the wife or girlfriend of a soldier buried in the graveyard. The young girl is said to have been so traumatised by the loss of her loved one that she committed suicide. As a result of self murder she would not be allowed to be buried in consecrated ground and so she could not be buried alongside her loved one. Her soul cannot rest in peace and move on to the next world and she is left to wander alone. The last sighting of this young girl was in 1977, let us hope that she is now able to rest in peace and this is why she is no longer seen.

I frequently get asked the question "why don't we ever see modern ghosts?" One answer I give is unless it is dressed in old fashioned clothes it does not 'stand out from the norm'. When we see a ghost our first reaction is to relate it to an every day occurrence -

this helps us to cope with what our eyes and senses are telling us. Only when an apparition is dressed in 'period costume' or walks through a wall do we realise that we are seeing a ghost at all.

Curdworth Church

5. A TELEPHONE BOX IN ERDINGTON ROAD

I have discovered on my travels that there are a number of telephone boxes scattered about the country that have reported strange experiences associated with them, but no more so than in the West Midlands, where I have found three. One in Bloxwich, one in Wednesfield and one in Erdington. The phone boxes in Wednesfield and Bloxwich are both reported to ring when you pass by. If you answer the telephone they are said to speak your name or say "I'm sorry but ---- is not here right now"

A modern ghost story is linked to the public telephone box in Erdington Road. A ladies house caught fire and she rushed to the phone box to call 999, to summon help. On returning to her house she attempted to rescue her family only to lose her life along with all her children. The figure of this poor unfortunate lady was often seen behaving in a wild and uncontrolled manner, trying desperately to make a call. After 1985 the old phone box was replaced by a new modern version and the distraught lady was seen no more. Where did the original phone box go? Has it been recycled, has someone purchased it and now possess a phone box with a ghostly history. Have you an old red telephone box in your garden and are you sure that it isn't haunted?

6. THE STATION HOTEL, DUDLEY

The building of this hotel was proposed by Wolverhampton and Dudley Breweries. The licence for the premises was granted in 1896 and the hotel was built and partially opened in May 1898. Alexander Smith was the first licensee from 1896 to 1920. During this period the opera house was situated opposite the Station Hotel which was good for business, until it burnt down in 1936. This gave 'birth' to the Hippodrome Theatre which was built on the site of the old Opera House. As a result the many famous folk that played the Hippodrome stayed across the road at The Station Hotel, three of which were Bing Crosby, and Laurel and Hardy.

I have heard a few ghost stories about this hotel, one of which is reported to be the Tipton Slasher who hanged himself in the cellar of the hotel after he lost his pub and fortune on a bet over a fight that he felt certain of winning, as his opponent was of a far slighter build.

Another story that I have heard is that of a hotel manager who

The Station Hotel

lured a maid down into the cellar in the pretence of fetching something, he made a 'pass' at the girl who rejected him and threatened to tell his wife. With this threat he panicked and battered the girl to death and hid her body in a barrel. However, the body was discovered and he was tried and hanged for the murder of the girl. The name of the murderer is thought to have been George, which is possibly why when paranormal activity is reported the staff say "George has struck again". On one such occasion two members of staff had moved some barrels to make way for a delivery, before going into the spirit stores (a room off the cellar). While in there they both heard the barrels moving in the cellar next door. When going to investigate they found the barrels had been sorted into sizes and neatly stacked in a different area to where they had just left them. When they went upstairs they asked the other staff "who has been down the cellar moving the barrels, after we have sorted them for a delivery?" To which they all replied they had not been into the cellar. On another occasion a member of staff was going down the cellar steps when he felt a slap on his face. He turned on his heels and made a hasty retreat. On entering the bar upstairs he told his colleagues what had happened to him. They witnessed a red mark on his face in the area where he had been slapped.

Is this ghostly activity in the cellar, the hotel manager trying to stop folk from discovering the body of the young maid he murdered and concealed in a barrel? Or could it be the murdered maiden trying to draw folks' attention to her plight? Is the movement of barrels in any way connected with the fact that a murder victim was hidden in a similar vessel?

The Station Hotel is now famous for its' haunted bedrooms. The main rooms that have experienced ghostly activity are rooms 214 and 217.

Two male colleagues were staying in the twin bedded room

One of the haunted bedrooms

214, when during the night one of them was awakened and on opening his eyes he saw a woman leaning over his bed. He tried to wake up his room mate, but without success. He surprisingly turned over and calmly went back to sleep. How he managed to do this I do not know. The following morning the gentleman refused to stay in the room again and asked to be transferred to another bedroom for the remainder of his stay. On talking to his colleague about his frightening experience, he was even more disturbed when he told him he had also been awakened in the night to see a lady sitting on a chair in a corner of their room. However, he also took no notice and turned over and went back to sleep. When people tell me about ghosts they have seen I never cease to be amazed how they so often just carry on with what they are doing or go back to sleep, although they might have just 'seen a ghost'!

A couple who were staying in room 217 woke in the middle of the night to see a man wearing a black hat standing in the middle of the room. He disappeared after a few seconds in front of their very eyes. Needless to say the couple were so disturbed by the spectre they had witnessed that they checked out early the following morning.

The chambermaids often complain because on frequent occasions after they have cleaned and tidied the room, when they give the room a final check they find the bed dishevelled, items such as ashtrays have been removed, and when they go to get a replacement, on their return the original ash tray is back in its place!

Night porters working in the hotel often experience ghostly activity. When walking around the hotel they often find cold spots, particularly on the corridor between rooms 213 and 217. When on duty the porters say they often sense that they are not alone – that someone is watching and following them. One night porter in particular seemed to be a target for poltergeist activity. Whenever he walked through the ballroom the optics would start to vibrate, the jukebox would switch itself on, and doors would frequently bang. The banging of doors is a ghostly phenomenon that is often heard by a large proportion of the night porters, but guests do not complain.

Different paranormal groups have carried out investigations at this hotel and have captured orbs on film and hazy mists on video footage. The Station Hotel never seems to disappoint staff or visitors

with its ghostly apparitions and poltergeist activity, so why not add it to your list of places to stay or visit, but make sure you have a 'stiff drink' before retiring.

Richard on the main staircase at the station hotel

7. DUDLEY CASTLE.

Dudley Castle

Dudley Castle has witnessed many traumatic and terrifying acts during its chequered and turbulent history. The first building erected on this site was in 1071 when the Normans built a wooden hill fort. It was massively re- fortified in the 12th and 13th Centuries in stone by the then owners the De Somery family. From them the castle passed by marriage to the De Suttons and in the mid 16th Century came into the possession of John Dudley Earl of Northumberland. In 1750 a fire started and burnt for three days, causing molten lead to run down the hill like an erupting volcano destroying much of the castle. Many servants lost their lives as a result of this fire.

On entering the castle grounds you first come to a small cottage on the right hand side. Evidence suggests that it was used as stabling before the great fire in 1750 which gutted the living quarters. However, after this devastating event the main purpose of this cottage would have been to provide a lodge for the Castle Keepers to keep a watchful eye on the ruins.

During Victorian times the cottage was home to a respectable family, until one evening when it was the place of a terrible mass murder. The father for no apparent reason lost control and murdered his wife and two children. This sort of event happened frequently in overcrowded Victorian slums when the man of the house spent nearly every evening in the local ale house, and then returned home the worse for drink. Research has been carried out on the premises which has uncovered a series of strange happenings. On one occasion a machine was placed in the cottage in an attempt to record voices of the dead. On later examination of the tape there could be heard very feint but recognisable gruff voices, which sounded like a man and a woman arguing with children's voices in the background. On another occasion a medium was investigating the outside of the cottage when he heard loud, deep growling coming from the interior. During later research it was discovered that during the 1950's one of the head keepers of the Zoo lived in the cottage and rumour has it that he had

The Cottage at Dudley Castle

a pet leopard!

Today the cottage still stands and strange events continue to happen, particularly as night falls. One Halloween evening a paranormal group were carrying out an investigation inside the cottage when one of them tried to exit the building through the front door. Much to every ones amazement the door would not open. No matter how they tried the door remained locked. The atmosphere within the cottage also became quite claustrophobic and some members of the group started to panic. They struggled with the door for three quarters of an hour when suddenly the door sprung open. The group fled the building never to return. On the very latest Huge Ghost Hunt that I conducted at the castle, the first lady to speak to me told me she had seen a bearded man looking out of the bedroom of the cottage as she and her husband were walking up to the castle. Her husband incidentally saw nothing. There was definitely no one upstairs in the building as the floors are unsafe.

On continuing up the hill you reach the outer gatehouse of Dudley Castle. In 1646 during the English Civil War a Colonel Levenson with four hundred Royalist troops laid siege to the castle. The soldiers had not been paid for six weeks. They had no artillery and were low on supplies. They needed to take the castle so a drummer boy was sent with a message to try and 'talk them out'. A single shot rang out and the drummer boy lay dead on the castle steps. This was considered to be a very serious crime as drummer boys were classed as

The outer gatehouse

54

being non combatant, which meant that they did not fight. Yes even battles have rules! The murder of this young boy was unfortunate as the 17th Century musket was considered to be the most inaccurate firearm ever invented. The ghost of the young drummer boy is frequently seen by staff and school children visiting the castle. Most of them don't report seeing a ghost, they just ask when the battle is going to take place as the have seen one of the re enactors by the gate. It is only when they are told that there is no re-enactment taking place that they realise that they have seen a ghost. Not only is the young boy seen but people often report hearing the beating of a drum which is heard quite clearly and then gently just fades away. The drummer boy has also been seen in the white building opposite the Gate House which is now the accounts office.

Other strange happenings are reported by staff in the accounts building. The temperature will suddenly drop and calculating machines start to work of their own accord. One of the staff was subjected to such an experience when on his own in the building that he ripped the handle off the door in his panic to get out! The gentleman concerned would not work in the building again without someone being with him.

The Under Croft is considered to be the most haunted part of the castle. There are no windows in this building so daylight never gets inside. The atmosphere is often described by staff and visitors as very oppressive. Light anomalies, poltergeist activity, whispering in medieval French and severe drops in temperature are just some of the eerie happenings and sounds reported by staff and visitors.

Situated in the Under Croft are two coffins, of which one is thought to belong to John De Somery (known as the robber baron). In life he was not a pleasant man as he enjoyed burning down houses if the occupants refused to give him money to upkeep Dudley Castle. He died in 1321 and was laid to rest in Dudley Priory. Many years later

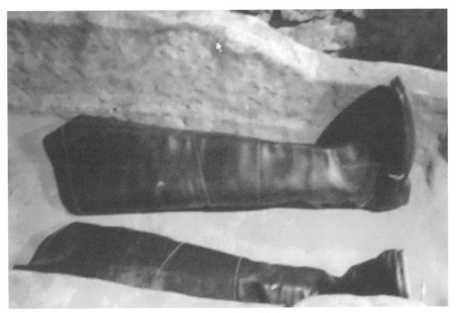
De Somery's coffin with boots

his coffin was dug up and brought to the castle. One day two sisters employed as cleaners were working together in the under croft when one of them had to answer a 'call of nature'. When on her own the other sister felt the presence of a person with her and on turning around she saw two legs standing next to the coffin, without a torso. The coffin thought to be that of John de Somery is in two separate parts. Is this why the cleaner saw half a ghost?

While we were filming the DVD ghosts of Dudley Castle, Dr David Dudley and I were in the under croft in total darkness, filming in night vision. It was so dark that I said to David "I'm talking to you but I don't know if I'm actually looking at you." When we completed our piece to camera and put the lights on he made a comment about the alchemist that also haunts the under croft and how many people have experienced a translucent blue light emanating from the fire place. The whole time we were filming in the dark I had noticed a bluish light around the area of the fire place and I had just accepted it and thought in the back of my mind that it was caused by the infrared on the night vision camera. It wasn't!

The Castle shop is situated next to the under croft and since the coffins took up residence in the building the shop has started to experience ghostly activity. Before Christmas 2000 staff were busy working in the shop when they saw a figure move across the room before disappearing into a store room. A few weeks later the same thing happened to two different staff working in the shop. However, the entry to the store room was blocked by a display of sponge animals, which started to sway as though someone or something had pushed against them in order to get through, but no one was there! The shop is also an area where poltergeist activity has been witnessed. A young volunteer was running the shop, she was all alone, suddenly the temperature dropped and the large key ring stand threw itself onto the floor scattering hundreds of key rings all over the shop. The girl was very frightened and refused to work in the shop again. The key ring stand is very heavy and has six legs with wheels and I have personally tried to push it over without success. A large proportion of the staff working in the shop are teenagers. Could this be why there is so much poltergeist activity happening in this area? Poltergeists tend to be associated with youngsters especially prepubescent girls.

The Castle Keep took fifty years to build and stands twelve meters high with three metre thick walls. This part of the castle was thought to be impregnable in times of siege and it is the last hope for survival for the occupants of the castle. Inside this building is the Garde Robe which served as the waste disposal chute for human excrement, and also sometimes dead bodies. Monks are often seen wandering around this part of the castle and could this be due to the fact that the walls were built from some of the stone taken from Dudley Priory and they have travelled in the stone --- this goes towards confirming my beliefs in the 'stone tape theory'.

The Sharrington Range was designed by William Sharrington in the 1540's and cost two thousand pounds to build. It provided the much needed living quarters and was the last phase of building to take place on the site. The Earl of Dudley who had this range designed and built loved to wander the rooms and corridors in life and his ghostly apparition is often seen by staff and visitors. Is he watching over the building that he loved so much which gave him his feeling of power and importance. People might ask why he should haunt Dudley Castle when he was executed at The Tower of London. The answer could be that he was so attached to Dudley Castle and loved it so much that his spirit doesn't want to leave and move on to another place.

The most famous and frequently seen ghost at Dudley Castle is that of Dorothy Beaumont (the grey lady). Dorothy lived at the

The Sharrington Range

Castle during the time of the Civil War. Her husband was Lieutenant John Beaumont who was Second in Command of the Castle

Garrison. During these traumatic and worrying times Dorothy gave birth to a daughter called Frances. However, the little girl only survived a few months much to the distress of her parents. They laid their baby daughter to rest in nearby St Edmund's Church in the centre of Dudley. Sadly not long after the death of her daughter, Dorothy also died. On her death bed she left two dying wishes. one - to be buried alongside her daughter in St Edmund's Church and two - that her husband be allowed to attend her funeral. Neither wish could be fulfilled as the Church was destroyed during one of the skirmishes, and her husband was not allowed to cross battle lines, for fear of him escaping to bring in reinforcements. So famous has her ghost become that the newly opened tavern at the Castle has been named after her. However, this tavern is now a place of paranormal activity. The alarms have been activated in the middle of the night for no apparent reason. During daylight hours the temperature will suddenly drop around the area of the bar and a strange blue mist appears and floats around. Is this Dorothy not happy at a tavern being named after her or is her spirit wandering around trying to discover why she could not be laid to rest with her baby daughter and why her husband never said goodbye at her funeral.

Tavern sign commemorating the castles most famous ghost.

In other words she has never been laid to rest.

It is no wonder that Dudley Castle is so haunted after the many traumatic events that have taken place within its walls - murders, battles, sieges, executions, accidents, torture and most of all death!

Richard and Dr David Dudley in front of the castle keep.

8. BADDESLEY CLINTON, KNOWLE, SOLIHULL

Baddesley Clinton is a wonderful medieval moated manor house parts of which date back to the 1300's. Many families have lived and died in this historic building wandering its' 'secret passages' and using clever improvisations to aid an emergency exit in troubled times. The building is now in the 'safe hands' of the National Trust and is open to the public Wednesday to Sunday—located north of Rowington Green, off Rising Lane on the A34-A4141. This is well worth a visit not only for its architecture but also for its' history and ghostly stories. When Baddesley Clinton was first built it was only through absolute necessity that you would accept an invitation to stay, particularly if the host had anything to gain from your disappearance. You may well find yourself disappearing down the

Baddesley Clinton

hidden passage that led directly without warning into the dark sewage infested waters of the moat.

This manor house has witnessed many happy and traumatic events as it's residents have come and gone, leaving behind tales of apparitions, poltergeists and ghostly events.

With the passing of time there have been many reports of manifestations in the house that support the idea that Baddesley Clinton is indeed haunted. Examples of these are the sounds of men's voices raised in disagreement heard coming from empty rooms. Footsteps echoing along the corridors, some running obviously in a hurry, whilst others are slow and heavy coming from areas of the house that are deserted.

The library which is often referred to as the 'ghost room' is reported to frequently have a very oppressive and overpowering atmosphere which becomes so strong that visitors and staff have to flee the room before they are overcome and collapse.

The family that inhabited Baddesley Clinton for the longest period of time was the Ferrers family who had the manor settled on them through marriage in 1531 and remained in their keeping until 1937. During their long occupation many strange and ghostly incidents took place and were actually recorded in one of the families diaries. One of these incidents was recounted by Meg Elizabeth Atkins in her Haunted Warwickshire 1981 "THERE IS AN INCIDENT IN 1884 WHEN A LADY VISITOR, SLEEPING IN THE TAPESTRY ROOM, WOKE SUDDENLY AND SAW THE FIGURE OF A FAIR- HAIRED WOMAN, DRESSED IN BLACK, GLIDE PAST HER BED AND VANISH THROUGH A CLOSED DOOR. THREE YEARS LATER THIS SAME LADY VISITED BADDESLEY CLINTON AGAIN AND THIS TIME OCCUPIED THE STATE ROOM. AGAIN SHE HAD A DISTURBED NIGHT, FINDING HERSELF SUDDENLY AWAKE AND THIS TIME

Baddesley Clinton surrounded by it's moat.

SHE SAW THE GHOSTLY FIGURE MORE CLEARLY SINCE THE ROOM WAS FLOODED WITH MOONLIGHT. SHE WAS CERTAIN THAT IT WAS THE SAME FORM SHE HAD SEEN IN THE TAPESTRY ROOM, FOR THE OVERALL APPEARANCE, HAIR AND STYLE OF DRESS, WERE THE SAME. THE FORM WAS STANDING BESIDE THE WRITING DESK IN THE ROOM AND SHE WAS FACING THE BED. HER FEATURES, THE VISITOR THOUGHT, HAD A DEFINITE RESEMBLANCE TO THOSE OF THE FERRERS FAMILY. AFTER A MOMENT THE FIGURE DISAPPEARED".

In the early 1900s Miss Henrietta Knight was staying at Baddesley Clinton when she was suddenly awakened in the middle of the night by the sound of many footsteps on the staircase outside her room. As the footsteps faded away they were replaced by a loud banging and the sound of fabric ripping. Finally most frightening of all when the sounds ceased she felt the breath of someone very close to her in bed—although she was completely alone in the room.

During the reign of King Henry V1 Baddesley Clinton was under the occupation of John Brome. He met an untimely death in London over a disagreement about a mortgage with a fellow by the name of Herthill. Brome's son took his revenge on Herthill some three years later when he laid in wait and ambushed him. Herthill died later as a result of the injuries that Brome had inflicted on him. However, fate took a hand and Brome returned home to find his wife in a compromising situation with his priest. He lost control and slayed the priest on the spot.

Are the ghostly voices raised in anger those of the priest and his murderer Nicholas Brome? Are the running footsteps those of Catholic priests trying to evade capture by Elizabeth's Protestant soldiers, by escaping through the secret opening in the manor wall across the moat to freedom? -- Who knows?

9. NEW HALL, WALMLEY ROAD, SUTTON COLDFIELD

The hall was built in 1126 and is the oldest inhabited moated manor house in England and as a result has many interesting stories about ghosts and manifestations. The building is a picturesque manor house that is surrounded by a lily-filled moat. King Henry VIII nearly met his death whilst hunting in the grounds of this old hall, when he was charged by a wild boar. He was saved by the quick thinking of a daughter of the house who fired an arrow and stopped the boar dead in its tracks. The King rewarded the girl by returning to her possession previously confiscated lands and gave her permission to use the Tudor Rose in the family coat of arms which later became the emblem of Sutton Coldfield.

Today you can stay in this lovely old building as it is now a luxury hotel which is filled with antiques that have been inherited from the many families that have previously lived and died in it. The hall is a romantic and historic place to stay where you can sit and

New Hall.

relax by one of the many open log fires. The hotel offers all of modern day facilities including an indoor pool, solarium, nine hole golf course and romantic four-poster beds. New Hall is ideally situated for the tourist wishing to visit Birmingham, Coventry and Stratford-upon Avon.

The hall stands in twenty six acres of beautiful gardens and it is here where reports of ghostly manifestations and experiences have been reported. In 1590 the hall was purchased by the Sacheverell family, from my native Derbyshire. The house remained in the hands of this family until 1897 of which the last member was John-de-Helay Chadwick, who enlarged the house and made many alterations.

Some of the Sacheverell family were suspected of conducting supernatural practices. It is certain that one of the family was an alchemist, as verses written at the time illustrates. A poem entitled 'Sacheverell's Warning' shows that this was George, given that he was the last survivor of the family. Another poem, 'The Alchemist of New Hall' describes a visitation from a demon, clearly indicating that there was a school of thought that considered George Sacheverell, (perhaps a member of The Hell Fire Club) to be in league with the Devil. Copies of both of these poems can still be seen displayed in the bar. These clandestine activities were always conducted in secret and the location of George's study is not certain, but when the passage, known as 'the screens,' at the side of the Great Hall was removed a room was discovered. The cob-webbed walls were oak panelled and this is thought to be the room where these unnatural practices took place. On entering this newly discovered room the builders commented that the atmosphere was cold, oppressive and intimidating. On numerous occasions loud crashing noises have been heard in the area next to the dining room. A resident was disturbed when eating dinner by these strange crashing sounds and she described them as "a large dresser falling over". These kind of sounds are very common in the case of poltergeist's. This is the same area where George Sacheverell's study is believed to have been situated.

The red landing at New Hall is said to be haunted by a lady in white and it has been suggested that she could be the angry wife of Henry Sacheverell who bequeathed the hall to his eldest illegitimate son.

Another of the ghostly stories is of a severed head that visitors have reported seeing rolling around the grounds, particularly in the area of the moat. This bodiless head is thought to belong to a servant of one of the Chadwick family who was suspected of being a Catholic spy during the 1745 rising by Bonnie Prince Charlie. This poor unfortunate servant had a major speech impediment which prevented him from speaking out and defending himself. The result was that he was found guilty and beheaded. His body was taken away for burial but it is reported that someone discarded his head by throwing it away. Somehow this callous, barbaric act resulted in the head becoming lodged in the branches of an oak tree. Soon after this ghostly apparitions of a bodiless head started to be seen. In 1827 estate workers were given instructions to remove any damaged and diseased trees. During the felling of one of these (an oak tree), a 'human skull' rolled out of the branches and crashed to the ground. Later the skull was closely examined only to find that its' owner had suffered from a severe cleft palate which could have caused them to have a severe speech impediment. Could this skull belong to the poor unfortunate servant who met with such a traumatic death? Until his head and body are reunited the soul of this poor man will never rest in peace, due to the belief that if the body isn't whole, then the spirit isn't whole and is therefore destined to go to hell.

New Hall's moat

The moat around this house is fed by seven different streams. Perhaps the apparition that is seen is nothing more than a recording. There is a theory now being investigated that water can hold a memory/recording in the same way as a D.V.D. or video tape. Homeopathic medicine retains the memory of substances that have been precipitated and removed from it. Is it the water in the moat that has recorded these tragic and traumatic events and is playing them back to us when we are 'tuned in'?

10. THE GATE INN, MILL STREET, SUTTON COLDFIELD.

The building that I visited on Mill Street dates back nearly 200 years and is believed to be an old toll house, hence its name The Gate. Toll Gates were established on major roads to collect cash for their upkeep. Toll houses were built along side them strategically positioned with windows looking up and down the road so the toll keeper could keep an eye out for potential customers. These unpopular buildings were often scenes of dispute as folk were angered at having to pay to use roads. Turnpikes trusts and local landowners could charge whatever they fancied, and the money taken should have been spent on repairing the roads. However, all too often the money went to keep the landowners personal finances in good repair. Sometimes in disputes gates were destroyed, tollhouses attacked and people were threatened with shotguns. Who knows what happened as a result of these frequent angry

The Gate Inn

confrontations?

The ghostly apparitions and phenomena associated with The Gate Inn is one of a cavalier. The landlady was working behind the bar when she heard the door open and close and she assumed it was her husband returning from his shopping expedition. On looking up she did not see her husband but a handsome cavalier. He was dressed in a very flamboyant way - floppy hat with large feather, belted sword across his shoulder and thigh length leather boots. She said "he looked as real as you and me". After about ten seconds he vaporised before her very eyes! She told me she was not at all frightened by what she had seen.

The toilets in this public house are haunted by who knows what. On one occasion a gentleman was in a toilet cubicle when someone banged loudly on the door. On opening the door no one was there. Similar occurrences are experienced in the ladies. – a member of the public was answering a 'call of nature', when the bolt on the inside of her toilet door drew back and the door swung open – to her astonishment no one was there. She could not explain how the bolt had opened of its own accord and she beat a hasty retreat from the ladies room.

As a result of these incidents the landlady called in the help of a group of local paranormal investigators to try and discover who was playing tricks on her customers. During their investigation around four a.m. in the morning, a six foot grey apparition appeared before the landlady and one of the investigators for approximately twenty seconds. Unfortunately they were unable to identify who it might be and the mystery still remains. However, when visiting this inn beware if you have to answer the 'call of nature' - you never know who might be in there with you!

11. THE MANOR HOUSE, WEST BROMWICH

The Manor House

A manor house on this site was mentioned in The Doomsday Book belonging to William Fitz-Ansulph, Baron of Dudley. Some of the building seen today has witnessed over eight hundred years of births, deaths, traumas, happiness and sorrow in fact the building must be 'soaked' with all forms of emotion from elation to despair. Some of the residents of the Manor House are the Devereuxs', Demarnahams', Freebodys' and finally came into the ownership of the Stanley family, Earls of Derby (through marriage). During their occupancy the gate house was added to the medieval hall.

By the 1800's the majority of the land had been sold to cover various debts, and the hall was converted into tenanted dwellings. In 1950 it was bought by West Bromwich Corporation in a derelict state. As a result of its poor state a demolition order was placed on this 'grossly dilapidated, huddle of buildings known as numbers 146-160 Hall Green Road'. As the demolition started the timber framed, medieval core of the building was uncovered. This resulted in a restoration and not a demolition programme where the wonderful old hall 'rose from the ashes.' It was during this demolition and then the renovation of the building that ghostly activity and paranormal experiences started to be reported. Demolition men and builders often see ghosts – is this because they are disturbing the building much to the annoyance of all the previous occupants!

The hauntings have continued to this day as the present owner, Pam recounted some of them to me when I visited. One of the most haunted parts of the building is the bar where dark shadows are seen frequently by the staff and glasses take to the air, smashing to the ground .When staff are on duty, alone behind the bar they are often subjected to a voice calling out their name, but no one is there. Footsteps are often heard on the ceiling above the bar. Part of the restaurant was originally the chapel, and a tall, gaunt, bearded man is

The Manor House restaurant

frequently seen peering out of one of the windows. A little girl and her grandmother are thought to have perished in a fire in the building and still linger in the corridors today. When Derek Acorah visited the building he felt that a great deal of the ghostly activity came from the cellar area. One afternoon Pam was alone in the cellar when she sensed she was not alone. She was so frightened, she was frozen to the spot and pulled out her mobile phone and called her husband at work- she just had to make human contact. On another occasion, about two years ago in the winter of 2006, when we had the first snow fall, Pam was in the restaurant with a visiting 'rep' when they both sensed someone else was with them. The 'rep' asked Pam "are we alone"? Pam said "yes." The rep replied "so who is that shadow over there?" They both fled the building and completed their

business outside in the snow. Pam remained outside too scared to return until a customer came and she had no choice but to return to the building. I also experienced the same shadowy figure when I was carrying out an investigation in one of the out -houses. The light shining underneath the door was obliterated by the shadow as it passed by. During this experience I also saw dozens of light anomalies dancing around the door. I have no logical explanation for this.

Haunted doorway

On a more light hearted

73

Richard about to enter the ladies toilets.   The infamous hand dryer

note I do have a logical explanation for the terrifying event which happened to me in the ladies toilets, which are reputed to be haunted. I was involved in a vigil when something spat at us. The result was screams, panic and men holding hands in a huddle in the corner. We discovered that there was no ghost just a perfume spray which worked spasmodically. We all dissolved in gafores of laughter at behaving like a 'big girls blouse' and I ended up on the floor in hysterics. I got my composure back, stood up and backed into the hand dryer which erupted and everyone screamed yet again. This was my most enjoyable investigation and I look back on it with great warmth and affection. However, it adds to my theory that eight out of ten ghostly experiences can be explained, but it's the other two you need to worry about! If you are looking for a good meal with 'real' spirits behind the bar then I strongly recommend The Manor House Restaurant.

12. THE COCK INN AT RUBERY

The Cock Inn at Rubery started out life as a farmhouse at which time it was customary for farmers to brew their own ale. The ale was then sold to the farm labourers and any locals who wished to buy. This selling of alcohol became a lucrative project and helped sustain a farm through difficult times. The farmhouse was situated on top of a hill, on the main road from Northfield to Bell Broughton, (which ran close to the drovers route from Dudley to Alvechurch and Redditch). Nearby was a watering hole at a ford on the river Rea. All these factors made the farmhouse an ideal watering hole for the cattle and their drovers. In September 1883 business at the Cock Inn had another boost when 'Black Country' workers came out on their Sunday outings to the Lickey Hills via the railway.

Today there are on going paranormal investigations being

The Cock Inn

carried out at The Cock Inn but up to now they cannot account for what or who is causing the ghostly phenomena that are experienced in the building by the proprietors, (Rob and Damien), their staff and customers.

A great deal of the poltergeist activity is prevalent in the pub cellars and consists of individual gas taps being turned off which causes problems 'pulling pints' in the bar. Staff are led to believe that the beer has run out so they go down into the cellar to put on a new barrel only to find that the gas taps have been physically turned off by unseen hands! Voices are also often heard coming from the cellars when nobody is down there.

A male customer was sitting in the lounge when a lady and girl appeared before him on the other side of the room. This was unusual for a woman and child to be in a pub on their own. He looked over to the bar to see if a male companion was purchasing a drink for them, only to find when he looked back in their direction they had disappeared. To have left the room they would have had to have walked close to him. Other paranormal activity reported is of candles extinguishing themselves, coughing, the sound of keys jingling, and the three resident dogs stand growling, with hackles raised looking into empty corners.

13. A HAUNTED BUS STOP ON COVENTRY ROAD, DERITEND.

Not only are phone boxes haunted in the West Midlands, but bus stops also have been sights of paranormal activity. One such bus stop is found on Coventry Road, where a railway bridge passes overhead. The ghost of a tall man, wearing a long overcoat was seen waiting at the bus stop at seven o'clock one morning. He was the only person waiting there. As the bus pulled in to pick up its passenger the doors opened and the figure vaporised in full view of the shocked bus driver. The driver was so disturbed by what he had seen that he had to be taken to hospital to be treated for shock. As a result of this ghostly experience the driver was unable to work for some weeks. Another paranormal sighting that is reported is that of a man who was thought to have hanged himself near the bridge after killing his wife. Bridges are used to cross over roads and rivers and may well attract lingering spirits as they may hope to use them for a different form of crossing over i.e. from this world to the next. It could well be the bridge and not the bus stop that has attracted the spirit of this man who committed murder and self murder.

14. THE WHITE HEART INN, WALSALL.

Around 1870 a grisly discovery was made in the chimney, in the attic room of the White Heart Inn in Walsall – a severed arm was discovered alongside a 17th Century sword. The arm is now in Walsall Museum. It is often referred to as a Hand of Glory. This is incorrect as a hand of glory was the hand of a hanged man embalmed in a solution of salt peter salt and pepper for two weeks before being dried in the midday sun. After this a candle was thrust between the dead fingers and acted as a talisman for burglars. The hand was supposed to open locked doors, render the thief invisible, and send the household into a drugged sleep,

A real hand of glory

particularly when these lines were recited on entering the building: *'Let those who rest more deeply sleep; Let those awake their vigils keep; Oh hand of glory shed thy light; Direct us to our spoil tonight'.* It was also believed that the candles flame could only be put out with blood or skimmed milk; Only then would the household awake. The one at Walsall was a complete arm and very small.

After its removal from the premises ghostly happenings were reported at the Inn. Staff and visitors first experience an icy blast and then a young girl, dressed in white appeared. She was often seen wandering around the premises sobbing and very distressed.

In 1955 the landlord heard sobbing coming from an attic room

The White Heart Inn

and went to investigate. On opening the door the sobbing immediately stopped. He turned on the lights and in the middle of the room, on the surface of a table covered in dust, was a small child's hand print.

When the severed arm was more closely examined it was thought to belong to a female child. Is the sobbing heard in this pub, together with the apparition of a young girl and the hand print in the dust, all related to this severed arm. Did a young girl have a traumatic experience in this place which led to the loss of an arm? Is she looking for it so her body is complete and then her soul will be able to move on to the next world and she can rest in peace?

Plaque on the ex White Heart Inn.

15. B.B.C. PEBBLE MILL, EDGBASTON.

Who would believe that the BBC's Midland's Flagship, Pebble Mill was haunted. Whenever I visited the studio to take part in radio interviews I was always met with the comment 'this place is haunted'. I was also surprised to discover that before the erection of Pebble Mill the area was a place where many folk committed suicide. Part of the site contained a hollow that filled naturally with surface water, creating a deep dark pool. This pool was drained in 1883 due to the number of folk who had thrown themselves into the waters and drowned. One of the last people to drown in this pool was Thomas Atkinson whose body was found on May 4th 1879. No one can be sure that he took his own life as Thomas was known to suffer from epileptic fits and some folk think he may have fallen into the pool whilst experiencing a seizure. During the building of The Pebble Mill

Richard with the discarded road sign found in a ditch.

The site of Pebble Mill

Studios one of the construction workers is believed to have lost his life. After this tragic death construction workers and security staff started to report paranormal activity. The atmosphere on sight would often change and workers said they felt uncomfortable as it would become quite unpleasant and eerie. An incident in July 1977 when the play 'Ritual of Stifling Air' was being rehearsed. Many of the cast experienced an extremely ominous atmosphere and strange, uncanny noises were heard. Later on the producer of the play discovered that the area where they were rehearsing was the same area where the construction worker had fallen to his death from some scaffolding

There are many reasons why I believe this sight may be haunted. The first one being that if the pool was a place where people committed suicide there is every possibility that their tormented souls would still linger in the area, as they had sinned by committing self murder that was punishable by going to hell for eternity. In the olden days folk believed in this 'mumbo jumbo' and as a result were terrified to leave this world and move on to the next. Suicides were not allowed to be buried in consecrated ground and instead were buried at crossroads, with a wooden stake driven through their heart. This burying of a body in such a place was done in order to confuse the spirit rising from the grave as it would not know in which direction to go!

Many haunted sites are situated near water, which may be in the form of streams, wells, dykes, pools, and would you believe toilets! Today many new ideas are being investigated where they think that water may be able to retain a memory, such as homeopathic medicine. The body is made up of about seventy five per cent of water and emits two kilowatts of electricity every day. This stored inner power is what is used in times of crisis e.g. when a mother is able to lift a car off her child that is trapped underneath which under normal circumstances would be an impossibility. In times of traumatic death the body gives off immense power (energy) which provides the conditions for a recording to be made of the event in the surrounding water or stone. At a later date circumstances might evolve resulting in a person becoming 'tuned in' to the frequency of this traumatic event which is replayed from the water or stone in the same way as we replay a film on our video machine.

16. THE GHOST OF RYTON BRIDGE.

Ryton Bridge still preserved under the A45.

The ghost of Ryton Bridge is thought to originate from the death of Thomas Wildey, a wool-comber by profession who is said to have murdered his aunt Susannah Wall and her daughter on May 2nd 1734. After being found guilty of the murders Thomas was subjected to the horrendous fate of being hanged and then his body was placed in a metal cage (gibbet) and displayed thirty feet high at Whitley Common where the crows pecked out his eyes

This all acted as a grim warning to anyone else who thought of committing murder. Folk believed that if the body was not whole and buried in consecrated ground their soul would never be able to rest and would wander the earth for eternity. On the Day of Judgement it was said that if the body was not whole then the spirit would also not be whole and as a result the person would be condemned to burn in Hell Fire forever. People facing death were not frightened of dying bur terrified of what they might have to face in their after-life. Would you 'try it on' at the pearly gates knowing you would not be admitted and go straight to Hell or would you stay here? Some of them have - including Thomas Wildey

Over the years the body decayed and resulted in bones dropping through the cage onto the ground below. These awful relics were often collected by souvenir hunters and made into such mementoes as pipe stoppers. The skulls were often removed and placed in museums on public display. Thomas's body remained on the gibbet post for many years until it was eventually taken down and what little remained of him was buried in the local

The Gibbet

sand pit. In 1793-4 the Holyhead Road Trust undertook the building of Ryton Bridge which was to be part of the London to Holyhead Toll Road. Sand for construction of this bridge was taken from the sand pit along with what remained of Thomas Wildey. This sand was mixed with other construction materials and used to make the base and joints of Ryton Bridge. Travellers reported frequently seeing a mist which seemed to hang over the bridge giving a very eerie chill to the night air. Toll keepers never stayed long in the job collecting money from travellers as they were frightened by strange noises, mysterious lights, and the prevailing mist that never seemed to disperse. These phenomena seemed to be more active around May the time of year when Thomas met his death. Many people believe

The Holiday Inn at the side of Ryton Bridge

that the bridge no longer exists and it has been said that parts of the stone from the bridge could be seen in the walls of the Ryton Bridge Hotel. (which became the Courtyard Hotel). I could not find The Ryton Bridge Hotel, I could not find The Courtyard Hotel, but I did find a Holiday Inn on the site, but no stonework to be seen. Undaunted I searched around and on walking through some trees, guess what? Ryton Bridge before my very eyes, with the River Avon flowing beneath. The original haunted bridge is hidden from above by the A45 and could easily thought to have disappeared- but no it is there for all ghost hunters to see.

Travellers today frequently report feeling uneasy when travelling over the River Avon in the area of the old Ryton Bridge or when driving around the Ryton roundabout. Many folk did not think Thomas was guilty of the murders and thought him to have been unjustly accused. Is it Thomas frightening the travellers as they go on their journey trying to get their attention, letting them know that he cannot rest in peace as his remains were dug up and disturbed and as a result his soul is left to wander lost for eternity.

17. WARLEY PARK/WARLEY ABBEY

An area of picturesque grounds/park is all that is left of Warley Abbey for the visitor to wander around and enjoy. In 1792 Samuel Galton 2nd and his wife Charlotte bought The Warley Estate. The architect Humphry Repton was requisitioned to design and landscape the grounds. He created a sheltered winter garden filled with exquisite scented flowers for guests to wander around and enjoy when visiting the house. Repton also created a wildlife area with a man made pool and he tried to ensure that visitors whether walking in the grounds or arriving by carriage, would be able to see the newly built hall from many different perspectives. However, Repton was disappointed when another architect, Robert Lugar was commissioned by Samuel to design and build the hall, which was duly completed in the gothic style that was so popular at this time.

Building material, particularly the stone, used to build Warley Hall was taken from the nearby Halesowen Abbey which had fallen into disrepair after the dissolution of the monasteries.

Warley Abbey

The ghostly apparitions seen at Warley Park (Abbey) are of two people - one female and one male. The female apparition is described as a grey lady who wanders the grounds. One of my many theories why somewhere may be haunted is explained by the 'stone tape theory'. This is where the stone of a building is thought to hold a memory of a tragic and traumatic event. Did this unhappy soul travel in the stone that came from Halesowen Abbey? – and as a result be nothing more than a recording, or is she the ghost of one of the Galton family who was said to have been a jilted bride, and as a result committed suicide. Is she too scared to move on to the next world, knowing that she is destined for hell fire and damnation because of committing self murder and so would never to be allowed to rest in peace!

The male apparition seen wandering around the grounds and woods is said to be that of a China man. The story behind this haunting has two different theories – one is that the Chinese gentleman was involved in the murder of one of the Galtons' heiresses and as a result his soul is too scared to move on to the next world because of the consequences he might have to endure for breaking the rule 'Thou shalt not kill.' The other story is that an old lady lived in a game-keepers cottage in the grounds and according to reports from the locals employed a Chinese gentleman who helped her with her daily chores of chopping wood etc, in exchange for board and lodging. He was said to be very happy and extremely grateful to the old lady who showed him a great deal of kindness. Does he haunt the area where the cottage once stood as he loved it so much he does not want to leave. We will probably never know.

It is not surprising that ghostly tales and apparitions exist about Warley Park as its origins go back to 1066. How much love, life and death, both natural and traumatic have taken place on this site, no wonder it is haunted!

18. ST. MARY'S GULIDHALL, COVENTRY

St Mary's Gulidhall

This building has been a witness to many tragic and traumatic events in Coventry city and is one of the finest medieval guildhalls in England. It was built between 1340 and 1460 and is believed to include parts of the 12th Century castle. It has had many famous and charismatic people within it's walls such as King Henry VI who used it as the hub of his royal court during The Wars Of The Roses. Mary Queen of Scots was held prisoner within its walls for three months. Charles Dickens performed here and George Elliot knew the building well and featured it in one of her novels. Another use of this building was as a theatre and was frequented by no less than 'the bard' himself, William Shakespeare. However, we do not know the identity of the ghosts who haunt this ancient building. It is very easy for ghost hunters to fall into the trap of identifying the ghosts with the famous occupants. None of theses super stars died in the building so why should they haunt it? They may haunt if they had a particular affinity or love for the building. Some folk say that the grey lady seen in the building is that of Mary Queen of Scots. I would not think that she had a particular love for this building or any of the other buildings that had been a prison to her for the eighteen years that she was held against her will in England. However, she is reputed to haunt many of these buildings. Some people have a presence and enigma about them and when entering a room they give off an energy and an aura that when they leave, you say 'they left a real impression on me'. Is it not possible that they can also leave an impression of themselves on the building. Another of the guildhall apparitions frequently seen is a man wearing a black skull cap, but again his identity is unknown. The most famous ghost associated with this building has only been seen once but has become a celebrity as it was caught on camera. The photograph was taken from the balcony looking down on a gathering of the Freeman's Guild in the 1980's. When the photograph was developed a hooded figure could be clearly seen standing to the left of the top table -- everyone said it resembled a monk, but do remember in medieval times most folk wore cloaks and hoods – yet again identity unknown..

Hooded figure top left of table

19. ASTON HALL, TRINITY ROAD,

This beautiful Jacobean Hall was built in 1618 by Sir Thomas Holte. The Holte family sold up in 1818 to a gentleman by the name of James Watt Junior. The Hall was purchased by Birmingham Corporation in 1949 and was officially opened to the public by Queen Victoria. Aston Hall was the very first large country house to be open to the public. This gave the ordinary working man and woman a chance to see into the life of the gentry.

Sir Thomas Holt's wife, Grace, bore him fifteen children - as a result she came to be known as 'Grace abounding'. However, Sir Thomas was not a likeable fellow and was renowned for his nasty and violent temper. At his previous home, Duddeston Hall, rumour has it that he stabbed his cook and disposed of his body by burying it in the cellar. Sir Thomas was not only known for cruelty towards his staff, but was also reputed to be extremely harsh towards his family, particularly Mary, one of his daughters. Mary was reputed to be frightened of her violent father and tried to escape from the house by eloping. However, he uncovered her plot to try and escape and as a

Aston Hall

result imprisoned her in a room in the tower. He kept Mary locked away in isolation for sixteen years when she eventually died, reputed to have been driven mad by her treatment and isolation. One of the ghostly apparitions reported by staff and visitors is thought to be Mary who is seen wandering the corridors and rooms. Is she trying to find a way out and escape to join her lover?

Another apparition that is seen is thought to be that of Sir Thomas's housekeeper, Mrs Walker. She has been seen on many occasions wearing the same clothes - a green dress with a high collar, and is now referred to as 'the green lady'. Today she mainly appears to the staff when they are spring cleaning or carrying out various renovations to furniture and decoration. The green lady is more frequently seen when the Hall is closed for refurbishment in the winter. Is she checking on their standard of work or is she trying to make it known that she doesn't want anything to change. Who knows? The story of the green ghost intrigued me more than most as from a child of four I have been frightened of ghosts. It all started when I played with older children. They told me ghost stories, including one about a green ghost who would come and 'get me' in the middle of the night. This story terrified me, I don't know why, I never put it into logical thought what this green ghost could do to me! However, as a result I never went upstairs on my own and my mother had to stay with me every night, holding my hand until I went to sleep. Even today I would not visit Aston Hall in the dark and I would never be brave enough to stay on my own for fear of seeing 'the green ghost.'

The third ghostly apparition that is seen at Aston Hall is that of a houseboy called Dick. It is reputed that he was either accused of theft or was rejected by a loved one causing such distress that he hanged himself from one of the rafters in the servants' quarters. It isn't known when Dick was born or when he committed suicide, but his ghost has often been seen swinging from the rafters accompanied by a sound which witnesses say is like a bag of sand gently swaying at the end of a rope.

Sir Thomas Holte disinherited his eldest son because he disapproved of his marriage to a Bishop's daughter. Without his inheritance the son and his wife sank into a life of poverty, causing them a great deal of suffering. What a cruel and unpleasant father and employer Sir Thomas Holte must have been. Does his ghost wander the corridors and rooms because his spirit is too frightened to move on to the next world fearing divine retribution and Hell Fire?

Aston Hall is open to the public and well worth a visit, not only to enjoy its' Jacobean architecture but also to listen to the staff who love to tell the visitor of their ghostly stories and residents just as they did for me.

20. TYBURN HOUSE, ERDINGTON

Tyburn House

Situated at the cross roads where Kingsbury Road and Chester Road meet is a pub called 'Tyburn House.' Years ago witches and suicides were buried and people were executed at cross roads. There are many reported sightings of a misty grey figure (neither male nor female) sometimes standing, sometimes sitting on a bench, seen day and night, always at the crossroads. In May 1817 a young lady by the name of Mary Ashford attended a Whitsuntide dance at this Inn. The following day her naked body was found in a nearby clay pit, she had been raped and strangled. A local bricklayer, Abraham Thornton was arrested for her murder. He was tried and acquitted. Many of the locals believed him to be Mary's murderer as he was found with blood on

Mary Ashford

his shirt. However, Thornton had a very strong alibi as he had been seen by eight different people at the time of the murder, three miles away from the murder scene. Mary's brother was so enraged by the not guilty verdict that he took out a private law suit against the alleged murderer. Thornton reacted by invoking an ancient law of 'Trial By Combat'. This involved him challenging Mary's brother to a duel of which he was fairly confident in winning as Mary's brother was physically impaired and frail in stature. Due to his physical weakness Mary's brother withdrew his prosecution action.

Thornton was still treated with contempt by many of the local folk who still believed him responsible for Mary's murder and in desperation he left the area and emigrated to America, never to return to his native shores.

Many years later - May 1975, another young girl, Barbara Forrest, was found in the same area, she also had been raped and strangled after going to a dance at the Tyburn House Inn. The final coincidence was that a man with the same surname as Mary's suspected murderer – Thornton was arrested for her murder. Guess what? - he was found not guilty! Were all these similarities just

Abraham Thornton

coincidences or is there a force beyond our control that causes a murder of a young girl to be repeated, with the suspected murderer being acquitted.

When I visited The Tyburn House Inn I spoke to Stephanie, the wife of the relief manager. She told me that staff have eerie and frightening experiences when in the cellar of the inn. Doors in the cellar have to be kept locked or they keep opening and closing with great force with no apparent reason. There are no windows or other doors that could create a draught for this to happen. A few days before I visited the Inn,   Stephanie was coming back up the cellar stairs with wine bottles in her arms when she sensed that she was not alone. When she looked up she saw a black figure that leaped down the stairs past her and disappeared to the back of the cellar, colliding with crates of bottles in its path. Over the last few years no less than ten different members of staff have experienced the same frightening meeting with a black figure, resulting in many broken bottles of wine! Upstairs in the panelled bar they also have problems with a door slamming closed on its own accord. They definitely cannot find an explanation for this as the door has a control arm which only allows the door to close slowly in order to prevent anyone being hurt. Is this ghostly activity caused by someone running through the pub to hide in the cellars to escape capture. Could it be the murderer of Mary Ashford looking for a place to hide – who knows?

Tyburn House at the time of the murder.

95

21. OAK HOUSE, SANDWELL

Oak House

Oak House is one of the finest timber framed yeoman's houses in the Midlands. It was built in 1590 and has mid 17th Century brick extensions. It is quite amazing that like the Manor House up the road in West Bromwich it has survived at all considering that it is in an area ravaged by the Industrial Revolution. It is believed that it is named after the large oak tree that stood in the front of the house until the last century.

The original owners of the house are not known but it belonged to the Turton family for over 130 years. When John Wesley preached there it belonged to a William Whyley. I wonder if Wesley sensed the ghosts in the building as he was fascinated by the supernatural and lived in a haunted rectory in Lincolnshire as a child and was terrified by a poltergeist called Old Geoffrey.

There is the ghost of an old lady dressed in black often seen by visitors and staff alike. She sits in a chair in the kitchen and stares at you as if you should not be there. The frightening thing is that she can see you, she is not just a recording but an intelligence. Children's clothes are frequently moved around and footsteps, coughs and ghostly singing are also heard.

22. COOMBE ABBEY, NEAR COVENTRY

Coombe Abbey

Coombe Abbey was built over nine hundred years ago and belonged to an order of Cistercian Monks. In 1603 the abbey was home to Sir John Harrington and it was in this same year that King James VIth of Scotland became King James Ist of England. Although his mother Mary Queen of Scots had been a Catholic James was a staunch Protestant. On his way to London James left his eight year old daughter, Princess Elizabeth in the care of the Harrington family. Life at Coombe Abbey was said to be beautiful whereas life outside the Abbey was often turbulent due to folk wanting the return of the Roman Catholic faith. It was during this unsettled time that the Gunpowder plot was 'hatched'. The intention was to blow up the King, his sons Henry and Charles, and all of Parliament in one go. Princess Elizabeth was to be kidnapped from the defenceless Coombe Abbey, brought up as a Catholic and married to a Catholic peer – hey presto what was believed to be the true faith would be restored to Protestant England. The folk who devised this plot were either related or friends. They acquired a lean-to building in Parliament Square belonging to Lord Ferrers of Baddesley Clinton near Solihull for the purpose of excavating a tunnel to gain access to the cellars under Parliament. As we all know Guy Fawkes was captured, match in hand, and so the plot failed.

On November the fifth in the early hours of the morning the news was received at Coombe Abbey of the uprising and that a hunting party was on its way from Dunchurch to capture Princess Elizabeth and gain control of the abbey. Sir John Harrington packed the princess off quickly to the safety of the walled City of Coventry. The Mayor, Mr Collyns gathered various weapons such as pikes, bows, and halberds, from the city armoury to defend the young princess.

One of the many ghost stories connected with Coombe Abbey is that of dainty running footsteps hurrying over the cobblestones in the old courtyard. Are these the footsteps of Princess Elizabeth encapsulated in the granite of the cobblestones, nothing more than a recording of that traumatic day, November 5th 1605.

Other ghostly apparitions seen at the abbey are those of Abbot Geoffrey, who was murdered at Coombe Abbey in 1345 and to this day he is said to be the culprit who throws glasses around in the banqueting kitchens and makes his presence felt in the old cloisters.

A green eyed gypsy by the name of Matilda, who was made pregnant and disowned by the master of the house, over three hundred years ago, sadly gave birth to a still-born child, and to gain revenge she put a curse on the family --- every first born child would have a tragic death! Although gypsy curses are not always taken seriously it is a fact that the Craven family, Lords of Coombe until the 1920's have had their male heirs die at a young age.

23. MOSLEY OLD HALL, WOLVERHAMPTON

Mosley Old Hall

This house was built around sixteen hundred for the Whitgreave family, who were descended from lawyers and M.Ps. The original house was a pretty half timbered building surrounded by dense woodland. However, today the timberwork has been covered over by Victorian red brick and the house is now surrounded by Wolverhampton. It was a member of the Whitgreave family that came to the rescue of Charles II after he escaped from the Battle of Worcester. He provided the hungry King Charles with a meal, a change of clothes and a priest hole in which to hide. The King laid in hiding in Mosley Old Hall for two days whilst he made plans for his escape to France. Cromwell's troops actually came and searched the house whilst the King hid beneath the floor.

The building is now in the care of The National Trust and is open to the public. One day when a group of trainee guides were on a familiarization tour of the building, when two of the group became very uneasy when approaching the King Charles Room. On reaching the door they refused to enter saying that they sensed some form of presence in the room. This story is even more believable because these two guides are reported to have not 'got on together' and so it is highly unlikely that they would have collaborated and made up the story.

King Charles II

The resident administrator, David Lee has lived in the hall for the last twenty years and told me when I visited, that objects frequently go missing and turn up in the strangest of places. On asking him if the house has a ghost, he told me of a story relating to one of his daughters. One day when they were talking about ghosts his daughter told him of a ghost she frequently saw in her bedroom. This ghost was in the form of a shadow, which she believed to be a man in his late twenties, who always seemed to be reading. He would remain sitting on her bed for anything up to two minutes before disappearing. His daughter said she saw him at least half a dozen times over a period of six weeks. He always appeared around the same time of day around late afternoon. She saw him for the last time around the end of July 1991. David asked his daughter why she had never told him of these sightings of a ghost before. Her reply was "there was no need to, as it did not threaten me and I was not frightened of it". David now uses this room as his bedroom but has never seen the mysterious male visitor. Could it have been King Charles studying maps in order to make his escape. I doubt it. The identity of the Mosley Old Hall Ghost remains a mystery.

24. LONG KNOWLE LANE, WEDNESFIELD, WOLVERHAMPTON

It is very seldom that you get the opportunity to visit a private house that is haunted and then be able to feature it in a book. Most folk are not too keen on the public knowing that they live in a haunted house particularly if they are considering offering the property for sale at a later date. Any way this is the story of what happens to the family living in a house in Long Knowle Lane. (written by the family)

"The house is a detached house built roughly in 1936, but before that it was farm land. We moved here June 4th 1988. At that time there were living here: David Maybury, Linda Maybury, John (3 years), Claire (11 months) and Sarah (11 months).

At first things were being moved, hidden or sometimes taken and never returned. Then the blame went solely on the children,

24 Long Knowle Lane, Wednesfield

although always denied by them. Such things that went missing at that time were: necklaces, cameras, small paint brushes and keys.

It was only after living here for 10 years that things more obvious started to happen that made us realise that it may be something more than meets the eye.

Most of the occurrences happened in the back half of the house. Mainly in the kitchen and bedroom above, although things have happened else where. First off while standing in the kitchen we would hear footsteps in the room above, we passed it off as John being out of bed or sneaking about but it also started happening when there was no one upstairs, this soon turned into running across the floor and sometimes ended up in something jumping on one of the beds. This was probably the most noticeable event that has happened. This happened quite a few times before anything else really happened and we could say to each other "did you hear that" or "did that really happen?"

In 1993 Linda's Mom passed away (June) and a new addition to the family arrived, Christopher (November). After this Linda kept smelling Freesia's in the kitchen which happened to be her Mom's favourite flowers, this happened on and off for several months. The next thing that was noticeable looking back was during the next year or two Christopher would never go to bed on his own and always came crying saying there were monsters in his room, and John had to go and lie with him to get him asleep. Sarah got the blame predominantly because she has an 'active imagination'. We only realised this a few months ago while talking about it.

Events seemed to calm down for a few years after that, until the elder three were going through puberty. The activity started again with the running upstairs across the floorboards and stuff going missing. New things also happened, in the main bedroom (Dave and Lin's). While in bed it would feel as though someone would sit on the edge of the bed. Up to date this has probably happened up to thirty times.

The next major thing to happen that is one of the most definitive things to occur was in about 1999. Dave and John were at the cooker cooking tea. Stood side to side about a foot apart and a knife that was on the edge of the cooker flicked up as if someone had whacked down on the handle of the knife, causing it to spin up in the air. It landed on the floor in between us both. In the same location not long after a fish slice was thrown from off the cooker at Dave and John and hit Dave on the leg.

After that we started hearing giggling, the first time this happened was when the girls were in 6th form and were coming and

The haunted kitchen

going at school. Dave was in the upstairs room where the computer is kept and heard giggling, thinking it was the girls back from school he shouted down to them "put the kettle on", only to be replied by silence. After a few minutes, (and being impatient) wanted to know where his cup of tea was, but only found an empty house. No one had been home that day. Not long after that John was due to buy a new car. The night before picking it up he put the keys and log book to his old car on the back of the sofa ready for the morning. The next morning when ready to go out the keys were missing. This was a regular occurrence, he always lost his keys, (or they went missing). Fortunately a spare pair was at hand. After a long search of the area we gave up and John went on his way. A few months later the keys appeared about a couple of inches from were they were left. There was no way they could have been there all the time because the throws that were on there had been washed and changed at least three times.

Not long after this John started going out with Laura who was 17. This meant that now there were John 20, Laura 17, Claire and Sarah both 16 and Christopher 10.

This is when it got interesting. On a few occasions we would have cold spots whilst sitting in the living room. An explanation for this could not be found as there were no draughts or open windows. We always try and figure a reason for why these things happen. Sometimes there may be a reason (if all else fails blame the kids). Dave has sometimes had the sensation of stroking on his face, and even as though an arm was put around his shoulder. On one occasion John got scratched behind his left ear and three red lines were visible.

Other things that have happened are small make up brushes going missing (also the smallest paintbrush of a pack would always disappear.) The first time this happened was when we were getting ready for a family party and Laura couldn't find her small makeup brush. We stripped the bed off in search of it but gave up. On returning from the party it was placed on the bed. Around this time Claire had an experience. While lying in bed she had the corner of her pillow pulled, she was too scared to look to see who or what this was, she shared the room with twin sister Sarah. She knew it could not be her because she had been fast asleep for some time. The rest of us were all in bed. Things gradually started to become more apparent and more frequent. After this things started getting quite scary. The next episode was on an evening, at this time John and Christopher were still sharing a room. Christopher was asleep and John and Laura were on their bed watching t.v. Christopher sat bolt up right in bed, looked at us pale as a ghost (excuse the pun) and said "where's that little girl ran to?" He then lay back down and went

back to sleep. As you can imagine John and Laura didn't have much sleep that night. During this time we noticed frequently that our two dogs Zak and Zuki would often sit and stare both at the same time and at the same place.

It was probably not even a few weeks after Christopher saying that that we had a reoccurrence. Christopher had his bed next to the door and was woke up by the light shining through the

One of the haunted bedrooms.

door. He shut the door but thought he saw John walking through the room going to the toilet. He reached and opened the door, he then turned back and said "sorry John" but John was in bed. This upset Christopher and also woke up John and Laura who were in the adjoining bedroom. This was also a long night. The last event was with Sarah. On a morning while doing her hair she walked out of the bathroom with a mirror in her hand. In the mirror she saw a tall

105

figure of a man. This was in the bedroom where the previous things had been happening. This really upset her as when she turned around there was no one there although what she saw in the mirror was very distinct figure. After this feeling something needed to be done as the younger members of the family were getting frightened we decided to consult a medium. We were recommended from a work colleague and gave her a call. We wanted to know if she could get it quietened down. We were told that there were three spirits here. A male and two children. They weren't here to harm us, the male was actually here to help with our health. This would fit with what had happened and we didn't tell her anything. It also brought to light a reason to why John would trip while walking down the hall now and again. She informed him that his old dog Sheena would walk in front of him to remind him that she was still about. Since then things have quietened down and we didn't have much happen, but things still happen. Actually a few days before writing this Dave and Lin were lying in bed and they felt something walk up the middle of the bed and Dave felt as if someone was massaging his back. This actually relieved a headache he had been suffering with."

25. HOLBECHE HOUSE, NEAR DUDLEY

"Please do remember the 5ᵗʰ of November gunpowder treason and plot. There is no reason that gunpowder treason should ever be forgot," (especially in the West Midlands).

The Midlands Plot better known as the Gunpowder Plot was originally hatched in Lichfield Cathedral

Most of the plotters were from the West Midlands apart from Guy Fawkes himself who was a Yorkshire man.

The gunpowder plotters.

Also many of the locations associated with it belonged to Midlands men and all of them are haunted. These include Baddesley Clinton, Coombe Abbey, Rowley Regis, Wolverhampton and one of my favourite haunts 'Holbeche House'.

The conspirators of the gunpowder plot fled from London when all had failed and Guy Fawkes had been arrested and headed back to the West Midlands and rendezvoused at the Red Lion on Dunsmore Heath. The Sheriff's of Warwickshire and Worcestershire had raised a posse of over fifty men and were riding in pursuit of the conspirators. This became known as the Bloody Hunt of Dunsmore Heath. The perpetrators decided to make a last stand at Holbeche House in Kingswinford. They did their best to prepare the house for a siege and told anyone who wished to make a run for it could do so by leaving via a secret tunnel which went to Himley Woods. Their store of gunpowder had got wet so they decided to lay it in front of the fire to dry. Guess what it was November the fifth and of course the gunpowder exploded! If only they had only been as successful with gunpowder earlier in the day. Five of the gang were injured and with the posse having by

Entrance to the tunnel still to be seen in the house.

now surrounded the house the men had little option and the cry coming from the house was *we mean here to die'*. On this cry the men charged out of the house, swords in hand, to be met by a hail of musket balls. The ringleader Robert Catsby glanced towards his friend Thomas Percy and whispered " stand by me Mr Tom and we will die together". The two men were brought down by a single shot, passing clean through one man before bringing down the other. Catsby although dying managed to crawl back into the house where he was found clutching a bloody image of The Virgin Mary to what was left of his chest. The actual doorway with it's original door can still be seen to this day. The musket ball holes can also be seen in the walls of Holbeche House.

A young groom, called Gideon Grove was severely wounded in the throat, whilst fighting along side his master. He managed to catch a horse and rode off through the fire and smoke and evaded capture fleeing into Himley Wood. However, he was eventually caught by

The conspirators were met by a hail of musket balls as they charged through this doorway.

the posse and killed. His body was left to sink into the stinking, festering bog. From this night, on the anniversary of Gideon's death, (November 7th) a ghostly apparition of a horse and rider is seen rising from the eerie bog. These reports are born out by the local farming community who report trampled wheat and broken fences without a reason for their damage. Sightings of the phantom rider include a description of him being dressed in thigh length riding boots, a dark velvet coat, mounted on a dapple grey horse, which appears to be galloping about three feet in the air above the ground. The sound of thundering hooves are often heard and a red glow is witnessed in the sky coming from the direction of Holbeche House. The house itself which is now a care home belonging to Southern Cross Health Care. For many years the building was an orphanage and is believed to be haunted by some of the children. Things often go missing and appear at a later date and a headless figure has also been seen. Is this one of the conspirators who still haunts this building which played such an important part in British History.

Holbeche House, one of the most historic buildings in Britain.

FURTHER RESEARCH

After reading this book you may wish to settle back in your arm chair, turn down the lights and follow in the footsteps of Richard as he completes his Haunted Tour of Britain on DVD and book.

Ghosts of The Isle of Man DVD

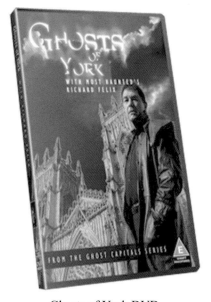

Ghosts of York DVD

Ghosts of Derby Gaol DVD

So you want to be a Ghost Hunter
DVD

Ghosts of Dudley Castle DVD

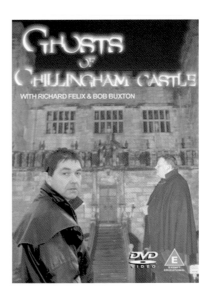

Ghosts of Chillingham Castle DVD

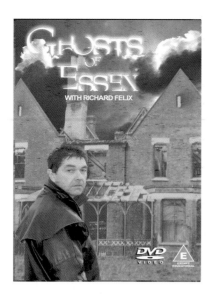

Ghosts of Essex DVD

Ghosts of Annesley Hall DVD

Ghosts of Gloucestershire DVD

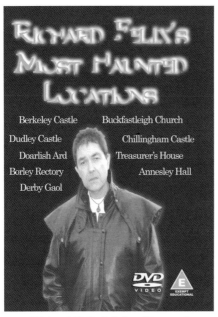

Berkeley Castle   Buckfastleigh Church

Dudley Castle   Chillingham Castle

Doarlish Ard   Treasurer's House

Borley Rectory   Annesley Hall

Derby Gaol

Richard Felix's Most Haunted
Locations DVD

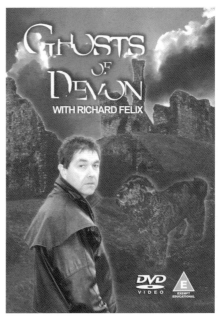

Ghosts of Devon DVD

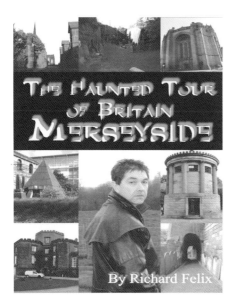

The Haunted Tour of Britain
Merseyside Book.

All DVDs and books are
available direct from the
producers,
Felix Films Ltd, Derbyshire.
Tel: 0845 88 22 782.
Order online at:
www.felixfilms.net
For information about
Richard visit:
www.richardfelix.co.uk